THE DECORATOR

THE DECORATOR

Florence de Dampierre

Principal photography by Antoine Bootz

RIZZOLI
NEW YORK

For George

ACKNOWLEDGMENTS

There are many people to thank for their assistance in putting together this book. Most of all, I would like to thank the decorators, for their time and effort. I would also like to thank Robert Janjigian of Rizzoli, Antoine Bootz for his wonderful photographs, and Paul Hardy for his superb design. Without Mark Lacava and Melissa Kilpatrick, the book could never have become a reality. I also extend thanks to Asher Edelman for his help during the last minutes of this project.

F. de D.

Rizzoli International Publications would like to thank Ann Dermansky, Alda Trabucchi, Howard Reeves, Jan Lindstrom, Charles Davey, Betty Lew, Mara Lurie, and L&I Color Labs, New York, for their contributions to this book project.

First published in the United States of America in 1989 by
RIZZOLI INTERNATIONAL PUBLICATIONS, INC.
300 Park Avenue South
New York, NY 10010

LC 89-45423
ISBN 0-8478-1118-2

Composition by Pub-Set, Union, New Jersey

Printed and bound by Toppan Printing Company, Tokyo, Japan

FRONTISPIECE: A view of Madeleine Castaing's apartment in Paris. RIGHT: A view of David Hicks's flat in London. OVERLEAF: A corner of Mark Hampton's Manhattan home on Park Avenue.

The interior design field is, first of all, a business. The largest of the design studios grosses over twenty million dollars a year. A firm will administer thousands of purchase orders for each project it undertakes. Thirty or more people are employed; among them accountants, design assistants, architects, and administrators. The "team" must work at full speed to maintain deadlines. Lawyers are always on call, drawing up sophisticated contracts. Reliable contractors—for construction, plumbing, electrical work, and the like—are a necessity for any one project, let alone the twenty or more that may be on a decorator's boards at one time.

Keeping up with the business at hand requires up-to-date electronic equipment; purchase orders are tracked on computers, inventories are stored via complex software systems. It isn't as simple as picking out a color scheme, choosing a few scraps of fabrics and some wallpaper, and just casually throwing a room together. And one mustn't forget the cellular telephone. Whether in the car or in a briefcase, this instrument is a decorator's lifeline, keeping a professional in touch with his or her office and clients at all times. (Many of the decorators have said that this particular device saves them at least two hours per day in effective working time.) Decorators' hours aren't fixed. They generally work seven days a week—shopping, traveling, courting clients, figuring out budgets. The profession is fast-paced.

Consistency is an important factor in a decorator's success, as is reliability. McMillen, the renowned New York-based firm which opened its doors in 1924, has been especially lucky in keeping a staff together. Veteran designers with twenty or more years of experience and established client relationships keep the firm's traditions going. McMillen President Betty Sherrill has been with the firm for more than thirty years. Designer Ethel Smith joined the firm in 1929. Vice president John Drews has worked for McMillen since 1959. That kind of loyalty is rare. For other decorators and firms, controlling staff turnover and presenting a consistent face to

clients is as important as controlling overhead. In order to find the right employees, train them, and keep them, decorators have spent more hours than they might care to remember devising employee bonus packages and retirement plans. Clients may come first, but design is a serious business.

Whenever possible, I have interviewed these busy people away from the bustle of their offices. In their own homes, life seems to go by on a higher, more Olympian plane. They could relax a bit and reminisce. But beyond these stylish private quarters, the day-to-day problems of the profession still linger. Decorators are often faced with the news that the crates of *passenterie* they ordered are stuck on a pier in Marseilles during a dockworker's strike, or that the delivery van carrying Capodimonte lamps hits a pothole in a Rome street, or that the lacquer on a Chinoiserie desk packed in the frigid cargo bay of a 747 landing in ninety-five degree heat in New York has basically disintegrated. Knowing that Mrs. So-and-so's curtains and sofa require the proper trimming, and that those lamps were a prize discovery during a buying trip to Italy, and that the exquisite finish on the desk was what made it so special, we can get an idea of the time, effort, and coordination needed in the decorating business. Decorators have to maintain a smooth manner.

The professional decorator is also a good judge of character. He or she must play a role requiring patience and a knowledge of human nature. Many of them cite a course in psychology as a necessary adjunct to training in design. The more gossipy side of the business is something they have to face, and they have got to learn how to "handle it." For instance, they may be confronted with this situation:

Mrs. X has a new apartment on Fifth Avenue. She has hired the famous decorator A to do the job. She would have hired the famous decorator B to do it, but he just finished Mrs. Y's triplex on Park Avenue and, you know, Mr. Y just sued Mr. X over that stock deal. Poor A, he's the fourth decorator on the job. Mrs. X fired the three previous decorators;

they just didn't make her apartment rich enough or different enough for her. And after Mr. X's takeover of that conglomerate last year, she's ready for the big leagues—but she needs a base of operations desperately. She can't have anyone to dinner, and she's beside herself. She wants the apartment to "scream" success, but someone told her that screaming isn't fashionable. Though the apartment is large, A is going to have to find enough shelf space for all those books, carve out enough staff quarters for the Xs' twelve maids, ten butlers, and three footmen, and create an intimate dining room that can accommodate eighty-eight for a light luncheon. And, it must be done in seven weeks!

It is rather unfathomable that a person with any sense would place him- or herself in such a situation willingly. Decorators are, however, a special breed. They can tone down a client's excessive tastes, creating a peaceful environment out of chaos. More likely, they can encourage and advise a client wisely in finding the correct style to reflect and enhance a desired life-style.

For people all over the world, a house is a precious commodity. Throughout history, decorators are the magicians who have transformed mere dwellings into homes. Sir Nathaniel Curzon (1721-1804) penned his sentiments about the importance of a beautiful home:

Grant me ye Gods, a pleasant seat
In attick elegance made neat
Fine lawns, much wood, and water
*   plenty*
(of deer and herds not scanty)
Laid out in such an incurb'd taste
That nature maynt be lost but grac'd
Within doors, some of fair extent
Enriched with decent ornament
Choice friends, rare books, sweet musi-
*   ck's strain*
But little business: and no pain
Good meats, rich wines, that may give
*   birth*
To free but not ungracious mirth
A lovely mistress kind and fair
Whose gentle looks dispense all care.

In today's hectic and ever-crowded world, a decorator's place has never been more valued.

F. de D.

KALEF ALATON

Brilliant simplicity

The spectacular design work of the late Kalef Alaton leaves a lasting impression. It is not that Kalef's interiors are overtly impressive or self-consciously put together; rather, there is a subtlety that comes through to make one realize that a master's hand has been present. At ease with quality and thoroughly relaxed, Kalef was an expert at mixing antiquities with modern elements in a stunning fashion. He infused his rooms with a regard for the quality of life he valued, searching the world for appropriate details to translate a client's personality into decoration. He aimed for interiors with vitality, a bit of whimsy, and a surprise here and there. Though undeniably glamorous and luxurious, Alaton-designed houses and apartments are notable for their refinement.

Kalef was born on May 14, 1940 in Istanbul, Turkey. He spent a memorable childhood with his younger brother, earning a reputation as the "worst possible student" at the French schools he attended. A daydreamer, he would imagine he lived in a grand palace, which didn't help his scholarship one bit.

He got his start in the working world with a job in his father's business, which traded steel, iron, and other metals. Kalef worked in Turkey for a few years until a relative from America came to visit and proposed that he join his family in the United States. Kalef wanted more than anything to go. It was like a dream come true. He set off across the Atlantic, visiting New York City briefly before heading on to his relative's house in California. He tried to find a job as a designer in Los Angeles, but was refused work wherever he went, despite his knowledge of European styles. He finally found work at a small decorating firm involved in the interior design of model homes and apartments.

This is how it all began, though he went back to Turkey after a year's time, vowing to return. In 1968, he moved to Los Angeles permanently. He found a New York partner, Janet Polizzi, and set off on building a business, establishing his special brand of decorating with an appreciative audience on both coasts.

When Kalef died in the spring of 1989, the design world mourned the loss of a great person and a creative force. His partners hope to continue the work of Kalef Alaton, bringing to clients the unmistakable style that made him so special.

LIKES: Beautiful objects, antique furniture, bronze

DISLIKES: Pretension, fakes

FAVORITE COLOR: Yellow

LEAST FAVORITE COLOR: Purple

IDEAL CLIENT: One who doesn't speak, except to say "yes"

WORST CLIENT: A French person

DREAM PROJECT: To decorate one of the beautiful houses near the Bosporus in Turkey

RIGHT: Kalef Alaton at his Los Angeles home.

A traditional circular Italian neoclassical table becomes an "arena" for bronze Roman figures of athletes and other antiquities. The masterful arrangement of objects was an Alaton hallmark.

RONALD BRICKE

Eclectic mix master

When someone describes Ronald Bricke's work as "sensational," it is not just praise bestowed for the way his rooms look. His rooms appeal to the sense of touch as much as they do to the eye. This tactility is achieved through the knowledgeable combination of surfaces and textiles. It is further enhanced by light, creating an invitingly sensual atmosphere. Within his rooms heavy velvets and soft satins co-exist, while a flutter of translucent silk transforms the flood of natural light through the windows. There is a spareness to the furnishings, with each piece carefully selected and presented within the space. His colors are strong and sophisticated, and he disdains "tricks"; if marble or gold are called for, there is no faux finish present. Ronald believes in the real thing.

Ronald was born on March 28, 1941 in New York City. His father was a butcher. For the first four years of his life, Ronald was raised in the Bronx, eventually moving with the family to Seaford, Long Island. Of good Irish stock, Ronald attended Catholic schools. After high school, he decided to attend the Parsons School of Design in Manhattan. Enrolling in the three-year course of study in design at Parsons, Ronald excelled, winning a prize that allowed him to study in Europe for four months. He traveled throughout the continent, soaking up the culture. Upon his return, he landed a job at the Yale Burge firm, working as Angelo Donghia's assistant. Donghia was an amusing and mischievous boss, but allowed Ronald to grow in his position. Ronald's

RIGHT: Ronald Bricke at home in New York.

first job as a designer involved the decoration of some children's bedrooms. Donghia recognized Ronald's talents, soon assigning him other rooms in the house to decorate. His excellent instincts and developing sense of style made him destined for success in the fierce design world of New York.

Ronald says, "You have to have nerve and a very strong sense of humor," to last in the profession. He can remember, for instance, a project involving the interior decoration of a rather large house just outside of New York

LIKES: Things that are light and transparent, the contrast between fabrics—like heavy velvet combined with soft satin, textures

DISLIKES: Plastic flowers, drum-shaped lampshades, indoor/outdoor carpeting, onyx, vinyl upholstery, faux marble

FAVORITE COLORS: Vermillion, violet

LEAST FAVORITE COLORS: Rust, avocado green

IDEAL CLIENT: Someone who has an imagination and a reasonable budget

WORST CLIENT: Someone who wants to pretend to be what he or she is not

DREAM PROJECT: To design a room for someone who is blind, where everything would have to appeal to the sense of touch

City. The job was complete; the husband-and-wife clients satisfied with the work. Their little girl arrived home from school, took a look at the new decor, and burst into tears. No one could understand why she was crying. Finally, the little girl said, "Oh, but Mommy, we have so much old furniture. Can't we afford to have some new furniture?"

A connoisseur of fine objects and a creator of rooms that are a pleasure to look at, Ronald has developed a style that is sophisticated, and definitely beyond mere "good-taste" decorating.

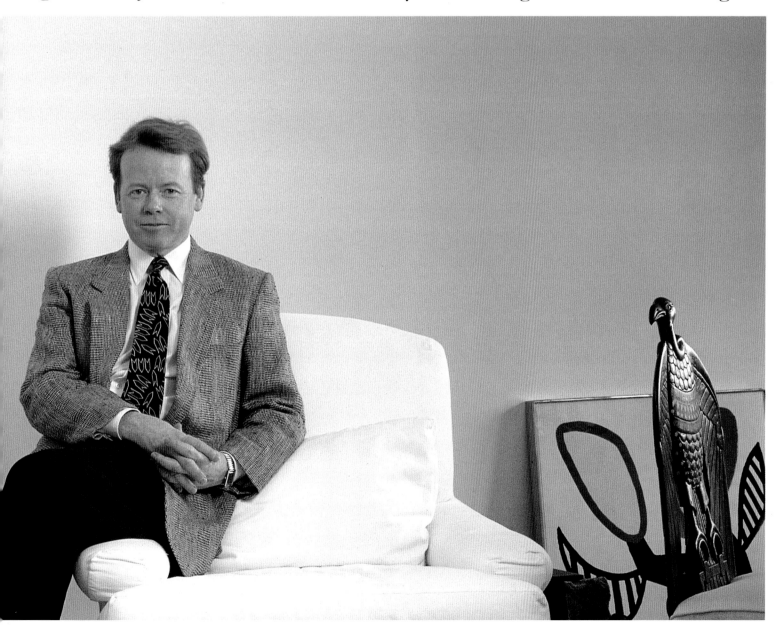

LEFT: Ronald's bedroom walls, painted in fresh turquoise and purple tones, enhance the airy feeling in the crisp, light-filled room. The bed features unique turtle feet. Ronald has the special ability of finding unusual objects to create wonderfully detailed rooms. RIGHT: On the contemporary stone table by the sofa, a Japanese-style vase and flower arrangement are paired with a bronze sculpture—a simple, yet effective, display. FAR RIGHT: The focal point of Ronald's foyer is an early eighteenth-century Dutch ebony-and-ivory inlaid table, in front of which, for contrast, stands a sleek contemporary metal stool. The floor is composed of alternating squares of dark and light wood—to echo the effect of the table's inlay pattern. BOTTOM RIGHT: At his Paris apartment, Ronald painted the walls in a faux parchment pattern to mirror the marble graining of the contemporary coffee table. The screen cleverly conceals storage space—every other panel opens as a closet. The lacquered bed, made of ebony and inlaid sycamore, serves as a seating area when Ronald entertains.

MARIO BUATTA

Chintzissimo!

Mario Buatta, son of a New York society orchestra leader, is one of New York's best known society decorators. "The Prince of Chintz" is a reigning king of English style. His exuberance manifests itself in rooms filled with a colorful, dense froth of patterns.

Born October 20, 1935, Mario grew up in Staten Island, attending local schools, including Wagner College, and decided to study architecture. But after nine months at The Cooper Union, Mario quit.

Decisively, he set out to be a decorator. A grand tour of Europe proved a revelation. It was the start of a love affair with all things English, "reeking of history, mystery, and romance," as Mario puts it.

Mario learned much on his trips to London, where he became friends with John Fowler and Nancy Lancaster, the arbiters of English decoration. In New York, he worked for Elisabeth Draper, Keith Irwin, and Sister Parish before opening his firm in 1963.

He strives to give his clients what they want. For a noted actress, Mario produced a green-and-white wallpaper speckled with blue butterflies. The actress chose it for her bedroom walls, windows, chairs. "I couldn't stop myself from telling her that if anyone was to come into her bedroom, they wouldn't be able to find their way out. She laughed and said, 'That's exactly why I want to do it!' "

Mario's social standing made him, along with Mark Hampton, a logical choice for the redecoration of Blair House. The two men worked with Selwa "Lucky" Roosevelt, U.S. Chief of Protocol. One decorator was constantly confused with the other. One day when Mrs. Roosevelt summoned Mario by calling "Mark," he spun to face her and bellowed back, "Eleanor." The misnomers ceased.

Mario prefers to keep his office small, working with two assistants. He dreams of retiring to England. He prefers not to dwell on the dreary English winters. He'll have a garden and it will always be summer.

LIKES: Flowers—especially tulips, portraits, antique shops, vegetable porcelain, white and gold period rooms, painted furniture

DISLIKES: Status symbols, Tiffany glass, Art Nouveau furnishings, plastic furniture, old houses done in all white, post-Victorian styles

FAVORITE COLORS: Blue, green, red, turquoise, Chinese yellow, jewel tones

LEAST FAVORITE COLORS: Orange and brown used together

IDEAL CLIENT: One who is trusting of my judgment and who can make up his or her mind

WORST CLIENT: An indecisive and impatient person who has too much money and little taste

DREAM PROJECT: To decorate his own place, so that he could actually have a real working house

LEFT: Teddy bears, suits, souvenirs, and fabric samples contribute to the "highly organized" mood of Mario Buatta's office. Mario is "captured" in action.

LEFT: A bedroom from a Manhattan show house features a grand canopy bed and a chintz-covered, extra-wide chair, designed by Mario especially for placement at the foot of a bed. RIGHT: Designed in the mid-1970s, Mario's bedroom includes a collection of Staffordshire dogs below a Chinese painting. The curtains, naturally, are chintz.

PETER CARLSON

The wit look

A sophisticated, slightly eccentric flavor characterizes the luxurious and relaxed rooms that Manhattan's Peter Carlson creates for clients. Peter stresses wit in his design strategies. He experiments with materials, sometimes coming up with seemingly outlandish ideas that are startlingly brilliant—"why-didn't-I-think-of-that?"—solutions to making a room exciting. In thumbing his nose at the axioms of elegant design and staying away from tried-and-true formulas,

Peter challenges established tastes. His imaginative approach, including covering a fireplace mantel with a live hedge, growing flowers out of the top of a coffee table, using sand to cover a portion of a floor at a Southampton beach house, is never stale, and always a source for conversation.

Peter was born in Boston on February 1, 1954. He attended Connecticut College, graduating with a degree in English and theater. At twenty-one, he moved to New York City, looking for work as an actor, taking acting classes, working briefly at Studio 54. Numerous odd jobs later, Peter moved to Connecticut to figure out what to do with his life.

It was there he decided to become a decorator, later moving his operation to lower Manhattan.

Peter's clients usually have a sense of humor about design. They aren't afraid to take chances. There is always a twist to what he does.

There are layers to a Carlson room. He utilizes fabric for its light-transmitting qualities, especially silk, to create an atmosphere of depth. Large- and small-scale patterns are used in concert, to liven things up and to shift the

RIGHT: Peter Carlson lounging in the bedroom of his comfortable Manhattan apartment.

focus from the details to the "whole" effect. Peter likes contrasts. He also likes comfort. He doesn't want clients to walk on eggshells in a room.

Eggshells are a source of irritation for Peter in general. He once got the idea to cover a pair of coffee tables in white eggshells. The project was in Newport, Rhode Island. Throughout Newport he could only find brown eggs. Finally, he found a source for the white variety, a nursing home where eggs were served three times a day. The eggshells were delivered to his office in huge plastic garbage bags. He spent hours washing them, eventually sending the

LIKES: Proper dining rooms, Mario Buatta jokes, lunches, good hardware, metal furniture, tall windows, wit and whimsy, jobs in warm climates

DISLIKES: Extension cords, foam rubber, too much jewelry, platform shoes, plastic flowers, most lamps, instant family trees and portraits, animal figure collections, eggshell furniture, nylon carpeting, velvet foxhead slippers

FAVORITE COLORS: Silvery lavender, moss green, midnight black or blue

LEAST FAVORITE COLORS: Florida tones: apple green and fingernail-polish pink, mustard

IDEAL CLIENT: Someone who has taste, knows what he likes, and has the money to do it

WORST CLIENT: A timid person with no style

DREAM PROJECT: To redo all the post offices across America, move to St. John in the Virgin Islands, move to a Venetian palazzo

cleaned-up eggs to Newport. Unfortunately, the tables these eggshells were to be applied to took longer to arrive. Peter ended up living on eggshells longer than anyone could stand, but in the end, the tables turned out beautifully. Artists sometimes do have to suffer for their art.

Peter's off-the-shoulder, elegant design style is decidedly upbeat. He likes a room to shine, often incorporating a "little touch of silver" somewhere in a room. Spare and uncluttered, his rooms are not filled with what he calls "small, junky objects," nor do they aspire to raise the social level of the client.

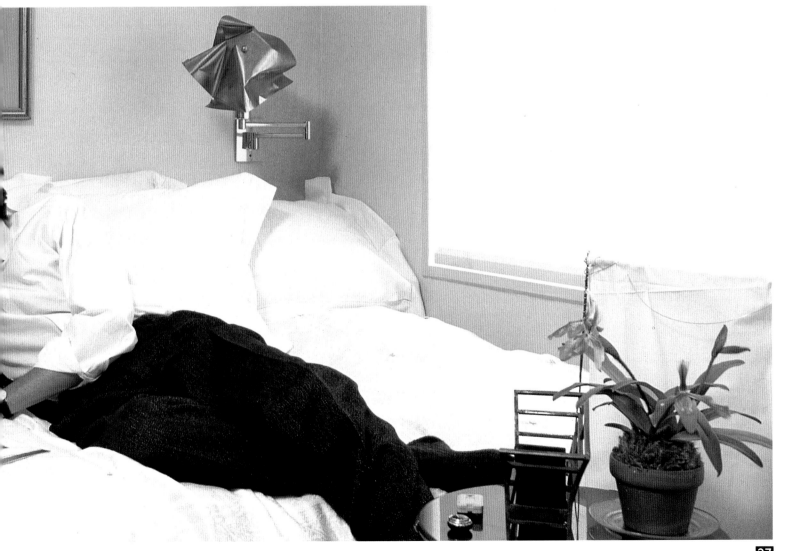

This Southampton show house room has an air of restrained elegance, and is both minimal and luxurious. A horizontal water channel and an area of raked sand were installed. The nineteenth-century iron day bed, the marble Greco-Roman-style torso, rice paper flooring, an eighteenth-century birdcage, and a turn-of-the-century painted topiary chair are combined to create a studied, surreal space.

LEFT: A regal apartment on New York's Fifth Avenue includes specially designed harlequin-patterned curtains, throne-like chairs, and a steel sofa of Peter's own design. The nineteenth-century painted wooden tombstone for a cat, inscribed with layers of puns, adds an offbeat touch. BOTTOM LEFT: In Peter's downtown office, he juxtaposes a French nineteenth-century gilt sofa with a contemporary mirror and standing lamp with a metal "crushed hat" shade. RIGHT: Pearl-dotted silk fabric, sheet rock walls, tea-paper floors, and a fireplace covered with heather-like foliage create a striking contrast of textures and simplicity of line in this New York show house room.

MADELEINE CASTAING
The grande dame of Paris

French decor has never been the same since Madeleine Castaing arrived on the scene more than forty years ago. It was Madeleine who extended the vocabulary of the French interior designer beyond the classical styles. She embraced a less formal look, used furnishings from periods long out of fashion, and imported furniture from cultures beyond French borders, notably introducing fine English furniture to the French public. These steps were revolutionary and can perhaps be compared to the development and effect of Christian Dior's "New Look" in the world of haute couture. French decoration, through Madeleine's efforts, became international in scope. The "continental look" was born. Though by no means a Modernist, Madeleine is a thoroughly modern woman with an up-to-date point of view. Her work and spirit have greatly influenced younger designers in France and throughout the European continent.

Madeleine was born in Chartres on December 19, 1894. She attended a Catholic school near Picpu in Paris. Married at eighteen to Marcellin Castaing, she moved to Paris permanently, eventually becoming the

LEFT: Madeleine Castaing in Paris. The mirror carries a lipstick greeting from writer Francois-Marie Banier: "Where are you going, beautiful?"

mother of two sons (she now has six grandchildren). Her husband worked as an art critic, so Madeleine was immersed in the exciting Parisian art scene of the twenties, thirties, and forties. The Castaings were also collectors—of Modiglianis, Utrillos, Bonnards, and Matisses. They could often be found at the Café La Rotunde, where they had a permanent table, participating in the contemporary French art scene of the pre-World War II years.

Through their friend Modigliani, the Castaings were introduced to the work of Chaim Soutine, a painter whose canvases proved to be a revelation to their eyes. His darker brand of painting excited them; it was so different from the more lively, lighter styles of the painters with whom they were familiar. Madeleine was attracted to Soutine's palette of colors and his emotional style. Modigliani was the shy Soutine's only link with the outside world. When Modigliani died, Soutine was alone and distraught. Though the Castaings had never met him, they made

LIKES: Proust, Celine, Stendhal, and Balzac's descriptions of interiors, English furniture, Russian furniture, Thonet armchairs, unusual shapes, antique fabrics, leopard skin, malachite, porcelain

DISLIKES: Modern houses with no "heart," decoration that is "heavy"

FAVORITE COLORS: Cezanne's blue, Soutine's green

LEAST FAVORITE COLOR: Beige

IDEAL CLIENT: One who likes to talk and talk and talk

WORST CLIENT: A French one

Madeleine's dining room table is always set—ready for the unexpected guest. Her table settings are a masterful mix of objects of numerous origins. The pinned tablecloth is a whimsical Castaing touch.

many attempts to communicate with him. Finally, they managed to contact him, eventually becoming close friends. Soutine ended up living and working in the couple's country house outside of Paris until his death in 1943. Madeleine's eye was forever changed through her relationship with this painter.

Meanwhile, in the mid-1930s, the couple bought the former house of Madame Sans Gene. Madeleine decided to make a business of selling furniture on the bottom floor of the house. With a stroke of genius, Madeleine decorated the shop, setting up the furniture on display as if it were in actual rooms. This concept was an immediate success, revolutionizing the manner in which people could purchase furniture. Madeleine emerged as a tastemaker whose design services were sought out.

When her friend Soutine died, Madeleine was left the bulk of his estate, consisting of numerous paintings. Not wishing to sell any of the paintings, and in order to supplement the family income, she went to work as a decorator full time, moving into new headquarters on the bottom floor of her post-war home in the sixth arrondissement. She continued to develop her distinctive style, which stood in clear contrast to the Louis style—commode-filled, Aubusson-carpeted rooms of classic French decoration. Her more lightly scaled mix of formal and informal elements stood apart, and creative clients were drawn to Madeleine's sensibility.

Madeleine's rooms are romantic, yet sophisticated. She is greatly influenced by literature and is known for using the colors seen in works by the painters she admires most—Cezanne and, naturally, Soutine. A house with no heart is a tragedy in her eyes. As in her own home, she selects the furnishings, fabrics, color scheme, and other embellishments to blend with and accentuate the client's personality. There are often zany touches to lighten up a room scheme. Warmth is added through the display of personal mementos and family portraits. There is never ostentatious display. Disliking decoration that tries too hard, Madeleine creates rooms that whisper rather than scream—with quality, a touch of the eccentric, and intelligence. A Castaing room is well thought out, and always a comfortable place to be.

LEFT: Carpets designed by Madeleine Castaing feature glorious adaptations of historical patterns. RIGHT: A Napoleon III chair stands in front of Madeleine's desk.

The blue-and-white sitting room has a Strasbourg
chamber stove as its focus. A nineteenth-century
Russian mahogany chair, covered in a rich damask,
stands at the left. An unusual nineteenth-century
barrel-back armchair from Vienna is at the right. The
classic mix of furniture and objects is a Castaing
trademark. The room was done about forty years
ago and yet retains a thoroughly up-to-date quality.

LEFT: The hallway of Madeleine's apartment, which is directly above her Paris shop, illustrates the "easy" transitions between rooms, and the casual, yet well-thought-out arrangement of furniture and objects.
RIGHT: Madeleine's collection of Chaim Soutine paintings is stored in one room. Soutine lived at the Castaing's country house for many years, until his death in 1943.

ABOVE: A beautiful floral patterned carpet design by Madeleine Castaing. LEFT: This passageway, leading to the kitchen in Madeleine's apartment, is not a public space, but is still decorated to please the eye, with the usual Castaing panache.

FRANCOIS CATROUX

Jet-set style

In Parisian designer François Catroux's mind, decoration does not have to be a permanent statement. An environment can change as an individual's taste evolves. And one look isn't for everyone. François could easily create period rooms, but his preference is for rooms that don't have grand aspirations; his look is more reflective of a client's self-confidence than a desire for status or false prestige. He steers away from stuffiness and what he views as the oppressiveness of historical accuracy. While respectful of the past, incorporating some fine eighteenth- and nineteenth-century antique objects and furniture into his design schemes, François is a "soft Modernist"—creating environments for contemporary-minded people.

Born in Algeria on December 5, 1936, François grew up in a family of wine makers. He disliked Algeria, moving to Paris at thirteen. He stayed in Paris with his grandparents at the Hotel de Salem, the official residence of the famous Legion of Honor. His grandfather was the head of the organization.

This lavish life was a culture shock for the young François, and he wanted to escape from it, too. At seventeen, he joined the French army, starting out as a sim-ple foot soldier—to his grandfather's dismay. After three years, moving up to the rank of Major, François left the military service.

Free to pursue life's pleasures, François became a "playboy," attending parties every night and generally having a good time. He ran with a fast crowd, the jet-set of the 1960s. In turn, he became what could be called an international citizen—jetting off to New York, meeting the crème de la crème in the worlds of art, fashion, and design.

In New York, he stayed with Alexander Liberman, the esteemed and well-connected artist and editor. Through Liberman, François made many valuable connections in Manhattan. His Paris base was an apartment his grandfather rented him, where he entertained constantly. In 1967, fashion designer Mila Schon came to his apartment for cocktails. After seeing François' home, Schon asked him to design the interior of her palazzo in Milan. The success of that design led to further work, as word of François's talent crisscrossed the globe.

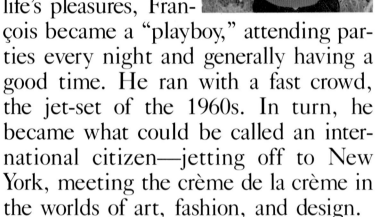

LIKES: Porcelain, going out late, fast sports cars, bronze, French furniture

DISLIKES: Anything coordinated, gold lame, chintz, a "well-done" sofa

FAVORITE COLORS: Beige, gray, ivory, black

LEAST FAVORITE COLORS: Purple, eggplant

IDEAL CLIENT: A trusting one

WORST CLIENT: People who are easy to figure out

RIGHT: Francois Catroux at his apartment in Paris.

LEFT: In the sitting room of François's Paris home, a bronze Atlas supporting an armillary sphere is on display. A French neoclassical secretary is at the rear, above which hangs a modern painting. A collection of Italian columns and various other objects are placed throughout the space. RIGHT: In Francois's dining room, nineteenth-century neoclassical paintings hang above a console. The photophores and lanterns hint of Francois's love of candlelight in the evening.

LEFT: Francois's Paris bedroom has a very clean contemporary feeling. RIGHT: The dining room table in Francois's apartment is luxuriously set for lunch. Neoclassical paintings hang over the carved marble fireplace.

ABOVE: A corner of the Paris sitting room illustrates the layered look that distinguishes Catroux interiors. RIGHT: Francois is a master of the combination of elements. The floor of the sitting room is covered with a unique marble-patterned carpet.

DAVID EASTON

The grand life

C hicago's Marshall Field's department store was decorator David Easton's first source of inspiration. David was fascinated by the four walk-through houses in the decorating department.

Born on April 9, 1937, David grew up in a close-knit Catholic family. He and his younger brother and sister were raised in York, Pennsylvania, traveling during vacations and holidays to Indiana, where his parents' families lived. At his Aunt Edna's house, David discovered photographs of a David Adler house, an eighteenth-century manor built in Lake Forest. "Once I had seen Adler's work and sensed its purpose, my life was set. From the third grade on, I knew where I was headed," David recalls.

David decided to go to Pratt. He studied architecture, finishing with a Bachelor of Fine Arts degree in interior design and the American Institute of Designer's Fountainbleu Scholarship, which took him to Europe.

David's work as a decorator is rooted in eighteenth-

century principles of the totality of design. He first experienced this design gestalt at a late August tea in a small chateau outside of Fountainbleu, served in a room with the French doors wide open to the fading sunlight and the leaves that skittered into the salon. That afternoon brought home to David the relationship between decoration, architecture, and landscape—the trinity that rules his work.

A scholar who taught a history of design course at Parsons for seven years, David translates his love for Classicism into elegant, ordered houses. His work is remarkable for its historical accuracy and the careful attention paid to craftsmanship and detail. His rooms resonate with visual charm and physical comfort, a

LIKES: Provincial furniture from France, Portugal, Denmark or Sweden, comfortable upholstered nineteenth-century furniture, eighteenth-century Gothic-revival furniture, painted and lacquered furniture, rooms by Adam, Cameron, Cuvillies and Schinkel, Ziegler, Ukrainian, Besarabian and needlepoint carpets

DISLIKES: Art Nouveau furniture, Postmodernism

FAVORITE COLOR: Red

LEAST FAVORITE COLOR: Blue

IDEAL CLIENT: Someone with a clear idea of what they want and can articulate about the direction they want to take

WORST CLIENT: An undiscerning one

DREAM PROJECT: To design a small pavilion house in Virginia

LEFT: Decorator David Easton at Balderbrae, his country house in New York's Hudson Valley. The "Great Hall" looks out upon a garden.

ABOVE: The terrace of a Lakewood, Florida, Bermuda-style house is an elegant place to lounge in the sun.

sense of ease and enclosure.

Before opening his own firm in New York in 1969, David worked with several mentors. Edward Wormley taught him the craft of decorating and the art of furniture design; Albert Hadley showed him the essentials of color and comfort; and Valarian Rybar, who worked in Mexico, Paris, and Nassau, allowed David to travel.

Through the years, David has developed his own working code. He believes in "living with a client," learning what his life is like, even arranging shopping trips to Europe where he can assess the client's reactions to decora-

tion, architecture, and furniture. With his meticulous planning and thoroughness, David's services are much in demand. Nevertheless, he has had his disasters—the 12' x 16' rug that arrives after a six-month wait measures 12' x 6'; he walks into a bathroom to find his client in the tub; the dog that was banished to the kitchen while the floors were being painted noses through the swinging door, adding his paw prints to the painters' decorative motif.

David works to please his clients and himself. He detests pretension, designer labels and nouvelle anything. Read Trollope he advises. "Money does not buy quality or life, nor does it ennoble the person," he says.

BELOW: At David's Manhattan pièd-a-terre, one wall of the bedroom is mirrored. On either side of the japanned Regency bed are Regency bookcases chock full of books, objects, and personal photographs.
RIGHT: David's Manhattan living room is furnished with many Regency period furnishings. The chair is the first antique David ever bought.

LEFT: The "Great Hall" at David's country house. The sconces used are copies of a Regency design in the collection of the Victoria & Albert Museum. Books are stacked on a pair of Regency bookcases. An engraved portrait, in a Flemish anodized black frame, is one of several in the room portraying French philosophers, writers, and noblemen. RIGHT: In the drawing room of a Virginia client's house, David had the trim around a Palladian window painted in faux marble, with elaborate detail. FAR RIGHT: David designed a chapel for clients in Virginia. Executed in late-eighteenth-century Gothic style, the space was inspired by the work of English architect Batty Langley. Pews and interior woodworking were copied from those at Shobdon, a Welsh chapel. The ceiling, painted by artist Graham Rust, depicts Virginia's founding and its history.

ABOVE: This English Regency sofa table, in David's Manhattan sitting room, can be cleared off for dining when guests arrive. The lamp is a nineteenth-century French candlestick, wired for electricity. LEFT: The "Great Hall" of David's Hudson Valley house is meant to be lived in. Floors are covered in waxed terra-cotta tiles. A nineteenth-century Dutch chandelier hangs above. Delft and other blue-and-white porcelain, collected over the years, punctuates the room. The mirror is one of a pair of nineteenth-century Spanish frames surrounding the original glass.

GAROUSTE/BONETTI

Barbaric sophistication

The interior and furniture designs of partners Mattia Bonetti and Elizabeth Garouste are enchanting, whimsical, moody, and offbeat. Since 1979, the Paris-based team has been stirring things up via their primitive rooms and furniture designs. The handcrafted quality of their work is appealing and easy to appreciate, though their clients are of a specific mind-set. One cannot be conventional in taste to work with this duo. Elizabeth and Mattia turn to papier-mache, rough-hewn woods, unfinished metals,

pottery, sand, and raw stones to create tour-de-force environments that look like no one else's. Their designs can be high concept as well as inspired by the vernacular. A faux-naivete is their sophisticated signature.

Elizabeth and Mattia began their collaboration as furniture designers. Their first artistic designs, completed without very much money, are testimony to their resourcefulness. To realize their paper projects, they would often go to Paris's Luxembourg Gardens to gather the necessary sand, stones, and twigs. The mothers and children who frequented the park looked at these two adults scrounging around for materials as if they were absolutely crazy.

Childhood memories play an important role in their creative efforts. Bold, splashy colors are used in surprising combinations. Their use of twigs, moss, bunches of wildflowers, scraps of metal, rocks, and earth bring to mind a youngster's backyard constructions. In some instances, their furniture's rough textures, played against one another, are reminiscent of the work of Isamu Noguchi; in others, a Franco-version of *The Flintstones*, with cartoon-character simplicity. Mattia and Elizabeth have recently ventured into creating pieces clearly inspired by the Gothic. Pointed arches and stained glass windows, though, are pared down. Though the design press was enthusiastic about Mattia and Elizabeth's initial furniture designs, the general consumer audience had a difficult time accepting their grass-skirted chairs and other quirky items. After about five years, their real break came. Superstar fashion designer Christian Lacroix invited them to decorate his new Paris salon. Lacroix, whose *pouf* skirts and rather *outré* outfits revolutionized the fashion silhouette in the late 1980s, wasn't afraid of Mattia and Elizabeth's eccentric aesthetic. With the Lacroix commission, their work began to be recognized all over the world.

Mattia was raised in Lugano, Italy. His family was in the antiques business. He studied the applied arts and textile design, eventually working in Lugano's silk industry. At twenty, he moved to Paris, designed fabric for the couture houses, theatre productions, and filmmakers including Eric Rohmer, the wunderkind of the French cinema. He met Elizabeth and her husband Gerard, collaborating with them on the furniture designs for Le Palais, a now-famous Parisian nightclub. With their shared aesthetic, Mattia and Elizabeth joined forces.

Elizabeth was born in Paris. Her parents owned an exclusive shoe shop called Tipbury. She attended architecture school at Camondo and married at twenty-three, immediately starting a family (Elizabeth and Gerard have two sons). In the early years of her marriage, she worked at the family shop, but when her husband, a partner in the business, built it up to extremely successful proportions, Elizabeth was able to break away from the shoe shop and took to designing wildly imaginative costumes for theater and films. She met Mattia, and the rest is a tale of creative collaboration.

LIKES: Everything related to the Tivoli garden, intricate art from Asia and Africa, painted furniture, music and musicians, art from the Middle Ages, photo albums, old newspapers, trains

DISLIKES: Television, Marie Antoinette's bedroom at Versailles, "recipes" for design, nightclubs, Victorian environments

FAVORITE COLORS: Turquoise, shocking pink, orange, purple

LEAST FAVORITE COLORS: Black, gray, beige—especially in combination

IDEAL CLIENT: One who trusts you, discusses things with you, and lets you create peacefully.

WORST CLIENT: A very strict person who doesn't give the designer any freedom

LEFT: Elizabeth Garouste at home in Marcilly sur Eure. RIGHT: Mattia Bonetti in his Left Bank apartment.

JACQUES GRANGE

Jacques of all trades

Jacques Grange's approach to decoration reflects the Parisian designer's *joie de vivre*. An unabashed romantic, Jacques applauds movies that move him to tears, vivid sunsets, and deliciously indolent weekends. He creates rooms grounded in nineteenth-century decorative traditions, but sparked by the unexpected. He deftly mixes colors, patterns, periods, and textures. The neoclassical style he often favors is colored by a modern sensibility. "Yes, I am very French," Jacques admits, "Even my clients in America are French-born or francophiles."

Jacques was born in the village of St. Amand on June 27, 1947. He grew up in Paris, in a family which counted many doctors on his mother's side, and engineers on his father's. He always loved to draw and began formal art lessons at the age of ten. When he was fifteen, his mother decided he should attend the Ecole Boulle, where he learned the secrets of lacquering furniture and selecting fabrics. He later attended Ecole Camondo, where he studied the history of architecture.

When he emerged from school, Jacques had a very solid foundation but no flair. He was shy. Then he met François-Marie Banier, a talented, very social young novelist who introduced him to the two women who would shape his taste, Marie Laure, Vicomtesse de Noailles and decorator Madeleine Castaing. Laure gave Jacques a taste for the palatial; Castaing taught him about the romance of design, the creation of a sense of intimacy. This aptitude for the grandiose and the intimate, for the luxurious and the humble is always present in Jacques's designs.

Jacques began his career by working with the illustrious Parisian decorator Henri Samuel. After a year, he was hired by Aaron Demachy as an assistant. For the last ten years, he has served as a partner in the firm he first joined when he was twenty-three.

Jacques carefully adapts his interiors to the architecture and environment in which he's working. In his own apartment in Paris, which used to belong to Colette, Jacques has preserved the flavor of the original decor.

LIKES: Columns, screens, comfort, bathtubs, scents, soft light, simple good food, to hunt for objects and antiques, ceramics, Jean-Michel Frank's work

DISLIKES: Acid-colored plastics, pretension, anything artificial, decorating "tricks," uncomfortable chairs and sofas, "long-haired" carpets, aggressive objects

FAVORITE COLORS: Saffron yellow, gold

LEAST FAVORITE COLORS: Turquoise, orange

IDEAL CLIENT: Someone like Yves Saint-Laurent—with a lot of taste and creativity

WORST CLIENT: A "pain in the neck"

RIGHT: Jacques Grange at his Paris apartment.

LEFT: The Christian Lacroix haute couture salon is an incredibly rich, whimsical design. The specially designed chairs are the perfect complement to the "wild" textured walls and painted borders. RIGHT: Mattia's Paris sitting room is very "undesigned," and serves as his laboratory for ideas. CENTER RIGHT: The *semainier* (a seven-drawer chest) is traditionally a vertically oriented piece of furniture. Garouste and Bonetti made this horizontal semainier, with different colored glass drawer fronts as a modern interpretation of a French classic. BOTTOM RIGHT: Mattia's drawings for the design of the Bernard Picasso château near Paris. The top of the drawing depicts the dining room; the bottom, the sitting room.

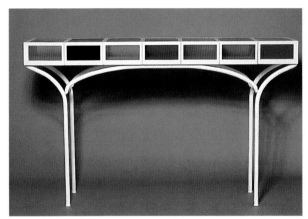

ABOVE: The Moon Lamp, a Garouste and Bonetti design that is often seen as a new "classic" among French designs of the late-twentieth century.

The sitting room of Elizabeth's house, hung with
paintings by her husband Gerard, is a comfortable,
casual place with the atmosphere of a painting studio.

CHRISTOPHE GOLLUT
Swiss precision

Warmth and coziness are the hallmarks of English-style decorating, while a formality and slickness characterizes the "Continental" European design sensibility. In the rooms designed by Christophe Gollut, who is based in London, there is a blending of the two aesthetics for a look that is comfortable to live in and appropriate for contemporary people who want to avoid extremes. Christophe likes houses that give off the impression that they have not been "decorated." He adores the Victorian period, with its emphasis on eclectic mixes of color and pattern, focused on pleasing the eye and creating a sense of romance. This human touch pervades Christophe's interiors. Though he might like to design a Modern house, he couldn't fathom designing a slick white-on-white interior.

Christophe was born in Switzerland on August 16, 1947. His father was an elected official in the Swiss government. Christophe attended a Catholic boarding school and went on to study law in Geneva. The legal profession was not his cup of tea, so he left school to at-

tend design school in London. He loved it. After receiving his certificate, he went to work for Alistair Colvin, designing fabrics by the yard ("The most boring thing in the world," he says) and selling furniture. Soon, a Swiss bank asked him to design their offices, which led to other jobs.

Christophe then opened his own shop in London, and clients flocked to his doors. What clients like about Christophe is that he is extremely organized about putting a project together, efficiently installing each piece of furniture and every fabric or wallpaper. Christophe offers a rare talent. Nothing seems to be forced or compromised—or too perfect.

In his spare time, Christophe retreats to the Canary Islands. His house there exudes a relaxed feeling, appropriate to the atmosphere of the islands. For Christophe there is nothing worse than a house without charm, wherever it may be located.

LIKES: Victorian houses, the international style from 1750-1880, light wood, needlepoint, antique fabrics, paisley, Fortuny fabrics

DISLIKES: Spanish decorating styles (with "long-haired" carpets, transparent coffee tables, and white sofas) bad lighting, Art Nouveau, English cottages with beamed, low ceilings, all-white houses, William Morris-designed fabrics

FAVORITE COLORS: Chinese-lacquer red, eggplant, Wedgewood blue, a touch of black

LEAST FAVORITE COLORS: Orange, brown, white

IDEAL CLIENT: A person for whom you have already done one house and they come back to you to do another

WORST CLIENT: The French—they know it all and want a better price

DREAM PROJECT: To do a new apartment in London for himself

LEFT: Christophe Gollut at his flat in London.

LEFT: Christophe used yellow tones to make the G. R. Flick drawing room in London a sunny, warm place. A portrait of King Friedrich of Prussia hangs above the Louis XVI white marble fireplace. BOTTOM LEFT: Christophe's previous London apartment, off Stanhope Gardens, had a "clean" Victorian look. In the foreground is a nineteenth-century Italian scagliola table with an unusual shell pattern. RIGHT: In the entrance hall to the Flick house are two Biedermeier side chairs, above which hang four eighteenth-century watercolors of flowers in extra-wide Biedermeier frames, a simple and elegant arrangement that isn't overwhelming.

Jacques's design of a sitting room for a Paris art collector is done in a palette of subdued colors—to match the gray sky of the city. A Picasso is hung over the Grange-designed sofa, with Grosz and Matisse drawings at either side.

LEFT: A spectacular orientalist sitting room in Marrakesch designed by Jacques for Yves Saint-Laurent, a frequent client. RIGHT: Jacques is an expert at creating fantasy environments, such as this Egyptian-style bedroom for a Paris client. BELOW LEFT: The "winter garden" room of Yves Saint-Laurent's Deauville house, which Jacques decorated with a light touch. BELOW RIGHT: A more formal approach was taken in Jacques's design for the drawing room of Saint-Laurent's Deauville house.

LEFT: The sitting room of this Paris apartment is decorated eclectically. Seventeenth-, eighteenth-, and nineteenth-century paintings hang on the walls. An ottoman, which can be used as a table, stands in the center of the room. A whimsical touch is the placement of a Louis XV child's chair in front of the white marble fireplace. RIGHT: A corner of Jacques's Paris sitting room illustrates the great care with which he chooses and combines objects, furniture, fabrics, artworks, and artifacts. His expert eye is present in every detail of a room.

FRANK GRILL

At the top down-under

Put aside the thoughts of Australia as a dusty, kangaroo-filled, surfer's paradise. Frank Grill explodes all the stereotypes. The Sydney-based decorator provides luxurious, grand, outright (not outback) environments for an extremely cosmopolitan clientele. Frank's taste tends toward the opulent and the expensive, with a color sense that is greatly affected by the bold Australian environment. Frank wants to use only the best. His eye for art and fine objects distinguishes him. Frank utilizes the advantage of living in Australia, with its relative proximity to Hong Kong, Singapore, and Thailand, where he often travels on shopping trips to buy furnishings "at the source."

Frank likes to "fight" the fashion of the times. He has been a minimalist, a fussy period-style decorator, and everything in between. He tries to be "of the moment," without being trendy, maintaining spontaneity with each project.

Born in Sydney on January 23, 1946, Frank was brought up in a house overlooking the ocean. He has one sister. His parents sent him to private boys' schools. Frank's family tree can be traced back to England and

LEFT: Frank Grill relaxes at Palm Beach—in Australia.

Scotland on his mother's side. His father's family has been in Australia since 1840.

Frank attended the University of Sydney. His parents offered him a choice of careers to choose from: doctor, lawyer, farmer, or businessman. He studied economics for two years, hating every moment of it. A third year was spent on the beach every day before he came home to announce to his family that he was going to be an interior decorator. His parents accepted his decision. His father, acquainted with the publisher of Australian *House & Garden*, asked the publisher's advice on how Frank could get started. At twenty, Frank was sent off to attend the New York School of Interior Design. He received his certificate, and went off to Europe to soak up the culture. He returned to his homeland, finding a position at a firm in Sydney. He learned the ropes of the design business, starting up his own firm in 1971 with James Gately, an architect.

LIKES: The penthouse at the Sherry-Netherland hotel in New York, spontaneity, Art Deco furniture

DISLIKES: Too many possessions, fashion, Memphis furniture

FAVORITE COLORS: White, taupe

LEAST FAVORITE COLORS: Purple, lilac

IDEAL CLIENT: One who trusts the decorator's taste and judgment and lets him get on with the job

WORST CLIENT: Frank Grill—he likes the best art and furniture and can never afford it

ABOVE: The sleek dining room of Frank's beach house is furnished with rattan chairs around a contemporary table. The marble floors are practical and luxurious.

RIGHT: Frank often travels to the Orient to collect spectacular objects, such as these pieces displayed at his beach house.

RIGHT: The Grill beach house is spacious and uncluttered—perfect for life by the sea.

ABOVE: An art deco console displays some of Frank's found treasures. He loves design from the 1920s—and to shop. LEFT: Frank designed his Palm Beach house to take advantage of the site's spectacular ocean views. The pool terrace dramatically hangs over the Pacific.

ALBERT HADLEY

Style with a capital S

There's room to breathe in spaces designed by Albert Hadley, a sense of what is correct and an appreciation of order. He's an editor, more interested in creating connections between a few choice objects than cluttering up the tabletops with a mass of things. His discriminating taste and crisp style have been compared with that of the illustrious decorator Billy Baldwin, whom Albert names as his inspiration.

Born on November 11, 1920, Albert  grew up in a splendid house in Nashville, fascinated from an early age by design: the setting of a table, the clothes that people wore, the houses that sprang up on the farmland near his home. His parents were both interested in furniture; his mother was a collector. During his prep school years, he spent the summer working at a furniture company and dropped in across the street at the shop of the best decorator in the South. He toyed with the idea of becoming an architect, carefully drawing to scale a house modeled after a *House & Garden* illustration he fell in love with. A teacher checked Albert's plan and found that the mathematics didn't work. So much for architecture.

Instead, he ended up in London with the United States Air Force, founded a batallion newspaper, and spent glorious afternoons with English decorator Elsie de Wolfe. Returning home, he set out for New York and enrolled at the Parsons School of Design. He regretfully declined the Elsie de Wolfe prize awarded after graduation; he didn't have the funds to go off to Paris for a year.

Staying in New York City, Albert taught at Parsons for the next five years and slowly began his career as a decorator. He was hired by McMillen, where he honed his skills as the only male designer in the shop. When he wanted to move on, he called his friend and mentor Grendo Van Day Truex, president of Parsons, asking for suggestions. "Do you know Sister Parish?" Van Day Truex said. "She wants to retire and would love to talk with you." In 1962, Albert went to work with Sister Parish. Today, he is president of Parish-

Hadley. Sister didn't retire though, and they have built a decorating "empire."

For Albert, a decorator's first concern should be his client's needs. "You have to be highly sensitive, to understand the person's feelings, what excites him," he says. Albert then designs his own interpretation. His happiest commissions are those involving old Victorian houses, bringing the past into the twentieth century.

A Hadley house is done in fresh, clean colors. His own living room is black and white. At the beginning of his career, he worked with a grand client who wanted white and ivory and various shades of beige. Unfortunately he was able to meet with his client only in the late afternoon in a room with very little light. The subtlety of the white palette was hard to see that day; it is found, however, in much of Albert's work.

A decisive man, Albert advises his clients to trust their impulses, to buy what they love at first sight. If you have to brood about a purchase, you probably shouldn't make it, Albert believes.

Whenever he can, Albert retreats to his house in Connecticut and works in his garden, compelled by the certain mystery he says exists there. His labors outdoors teach patience, he says.

LIKES: Things that have a personal meaning, old Victorian homes

DISLIKES: A lack of decision in others or in himself.

FAVORITE COLORS: Black, white, ivory

LEAST FAVORITE COLORS: Turquoise with brown and orange

IDEAL CLIENT: Secure, fashionable, educated, enthusiastic, knowledgeable, and rich!

WORST CLIENT: Competitive, not sure of their own identity, and cares too much about what others think

DREAM PROJECT: To have a bulldozer to get a beautiful garden organized

BELOW: Decorator Albert Hadley at home in Manhattan. The walls are covered with silver tea paper. A painting by Helene Fessenmaier hangs above the sofa. The French Louis XVI provincial chair is one of a set of four.

RIGHT: In a corner of Albert's apartment, framed artworks cover the walls. The Louis XVI chair is one of a set of six that once belonged to William Odom, the director of the Parsons School of Design. The paper star was a gift from young decorators Jeff Bilhuber and Tom Scheerer, and the metal sculpture is from Japan.

RIGHT: Albert loves chairs, seeing them as sculptural objects. This hallway in Albert's Manhattan apartment, with black lacquer strie walls, has, as its focus, a very rare English mahogany hall chair, purchased years ago. The collection of photographs of Richard Hambelton's shadow figures, is by Dennis Krukowski. The gilt mirror was a gift.

LEFT: Albert expertly puts together pieces from many eras. In this corner of his bedroom, a Chinese lacquer screen and metal stool surround his bedside table, cluttered with the "tools" of his life. The hand sculpture is by Karl Springer.

RIGHT: A bulletin board dominates Albert's sitting room. On it are arranged numerous photographs, postcards, objects, and newspaper clippings that have a special meaning to him. On the black lacquer table in front of this "wall of memories" are an early Giacometti lamp, a nail ball (a gift from the late decorator Billy Baldwin), and a pair of bronze diving boys by Fazzini.

ABOVE: On the fireplace mantel in his bedroom, Albert has arranged a striking "skyline" of found objects and souvenirs from friends.
ABOVE RIGHT: The English wooden basket, filled with logs, has a very strong sculptural quality. Every part of Albert's apartment is artistically "composed."

ABOVE: A nineteenth-century copy of a bust in the Cluny Museum peers over the sitting room of Albert's apartment. The silver-leaf coffee table is a reproduction of a Jean-Michel Frank design. The original Frank table, covered in parchment, was given to Albert by Mrs. Brown of McMillen. He had the copy made, passing the original on to young decorator Gary Hager.

GARY HAGER

A *new viewpoint*

A room, in young Parish-Hadley decorator Gary Hager's mind, should be quiet and peaceful—a tranquil place that is relaxed and comfortable. Gary's designs are subtle. He stays away from strong statements of color, the fussiness of by-the-book decorating schemes, and fashionable solutions. His updated, softly eclectic look fits in with the Parish-Hadley tradition. He is intolerant of low-quality furniture and objects, and is versatile in his choice of furnishings, from stately English pieces to Modern classics from the 1920s and 1930s.

Gary was born in Buffalo, New York on September 7, 1951. His father was an antique dealer in East Aurora, New York, a center for the production of furniture in the Arts & Crafts style of the early twentieth century. He and his three brothers and one sister grew up in a "wonderful" nineteenth-century house. Gary went on to attend Hobart College, graduating in 1973. He spent the senior year of his undergraduate education studying in Paris. Returning from Europe, he settled in Manhattan, working at a restaurant called La Petite

Ferme. He moved on to a job at the Boxtree, another Manhattan eatery, where he eventually was made maître d'. He gave up on New York, moving to San Francisco to run a restaurant there. In 1977, however, he decided the restaurant business wasn't for him, and returned to Manhattan. He was interested in design, so he managed to get an interview with Albert Hadley, who hired Gary as a driver (for two weeks). He then moved on to the assistant level, with responsibilities he describes as "a little bit of everything." After six years with the firm, he was given his own clients to handle.

Gary is a collector with a special fondness for good chair designs. He encourages clients in their particular areas of interest. "People should never be afraid to be themselves," he states.

Gary believes in decoration that is intelligently composed, not frivolous or overbearing, and has a gentility about it that can create the right environment for the "good life."

LIKES: Pictures and picture frames, Louis XVI furniture, "good" American pottery, "good" linens, gold, the beach, hunting for antiques, the Arts & Crafts movement, Directoire furniture, Scottish furniture, cats, chair collections

DISLIKES: Vertical blinds, things that are "in," sloppiness, fussy apartments, Art Nouveau, Tiffany lamps, period rooms

FAVORITE COLORS: Green—especially blue-green, muted shades

LEAST FAVORITE COLORS: Acid colors, orange

IDEAL CLIENT: A knowledgeable, intelligent person who isn't afraid to be himself

WORST CLIENT: A selfish person

LEFT: Parish-Hadley decorator Gary Hager at home in New York. Over his shoulder, a William Auerbach Levy painting of a young man, circa 1948.

RIGHT: Gary expertly worked with a collector of Arts & Crafts furniture in creating the proper ambience for this New York apartment. The fireplace is Rookwood tile, and the painting is by Buffalo, New York artist Charles Burchfield. FAR RIGHT: The Arts & Crafts period is one of Gary's favorites. At a collector's apartment, a Roycroft organizer and an Arts & Crafts chair are harmoniously paired.

RIGHT: An Elliot Levine painting hangs in the living room of Gary's New York apartment. The table is English Regency.

LEFT: At an apartment on New York's Upper West Side, Gary placed a Japanese screen above an L. and J. G. Stickley settle. RIGHT: In a New York apartment, Gary again shows his talent for combining seemingly incongruous furnishings successfully. A Miró sculpture, a French nineteenth-century Impressionist painting, and a French Louis XV bergere seem to belong together. BELOW: The entrance hall of Gary's first New York apartment. The chair is Directoire; inside hangs a Jean-Michel Frank mirror. One can see Albert Hadley's influence on Gary's design aesthetic.

ANTHONY HAIL

All the right moves

San Francisco is a sophisticated town, full of people with refined tastes who enjoy a life-style that is both formal and relaxed. A designer must contend with history as well as new trends. Enter Anthony Hail, the toast of San Francisco's tastemakers.

Tony offers his clients not the super-relaxed style associated with the "California look," but rather stately, formal, nineteenth-century-style interiors. There is also a touch of the dramatic to Tony's

interior design work.

Born in Houston on October 23, 1924, Tony is from a family that hailed from Tennessee. When he was young, his mother remarried a Danish man. He went to live in Denmark for many years. The experience of living in Europe greatly affected Tony's aesthetic, and to this day, his rooms reflect the understated style of Scandinavia.

Tony attended college at Washington & Lee, going on to study architecture at Harvard. Soon afterward, he got his first big break. President Harry Truman and First Lady Bess were hiring architects to redecorate The White House. Tony was among those selected. He moved on to California, where in San Francisco he met Michael Taylor, another decorator. The two men got along grandly, and became partners. Tony cites his success among San Francisco's social elite to the fact that a lot of very influential women were attracted to his charming personality and gave him work. His success, however, was not disaster-free.

LIKES: Danish furniture and art, decorative screens
DISLIKES: Pianos, fake Oriental rugs, gladiolas, pretension
FAVORITE COLORS: Cranberry, celery green
LEAST FAVORITE COLORS: Puce, liver
IDEAL CLIENT: Someone who knows how to listen
WORST CLIENT: A penny-pincher

Years ago, Tony was supposed to "take care of" a lady client of Billy Baldwin, the New York decorator, who'd "organized" some curtains for the woman's San Francisco home. The curtains were installed. The client phoned. The bottoms of the curtains, which had just touched the floor, were now fifteen inches above it. The next day, the curtains were too long. Tony finally realized that the curtains were hung next to a heater and an air conditioner. The climate of San Francisco necessitated the use of heating and cooling equipment, affecting the fabric. With that knowledge, Tony changed them entirely. He learned that to become a successful decorator, you have to be part technician.

BELOW LEFT: Tony Hail in the bedroom of his San Francisco house.
BELOW: A travel *necessaire* is on display in Tony's bedroom. The table is Swedish Louis XVI, one of his favorite periods.

LEFT: The chic Louis Vuitton trunk and suitcases, on display in the decorator's bedroom, hint of the grand old days Tony spent as a world traveler. Artworks hang above, in a studied, yet warmly cluttered arrangement. RIGHT: Tony's elegant bedroom has a classic Louis XVI bed at its heart. The room is comfortable, with just a touch of formality—Tony's trademark.

MARK HAMPTON

An American classic

Most boys dream of being baseball players or firemen when they grow up. Mark Hampton always wanted to be a decorator. But while working the farms that surrounded his hometown of Plainfield, Indiana, he could scarcely have imagined the extraordinary success he would enjoy in his chosen profession. His clients include three presidents, illustrious museums and universities, and a long list of socially prominent people. He's a hot ticket on the lecture circuit, a much-published author, and an artist whose watercolors are exhibited in major New York City and London art galleries.

Born on June 1, 1940, Mark and his sister grew up in a small Midwestern town, members of a Quaker farming family. He recalls that his early idols were Le Corbusier, Frank Lloyd Wright, and Philip Johnson. He did his undergraduate work at DePauw University and the London School of Economics; holder of a Ford Fellowship, he earned a Master of Fine Arts degree from New York University.

During the early years of his career, Mark served as an assistant at three distinguished firms. He started out in London with David Hicks, and later worked with Sister Parish and McMillen. In the late 1960s, he ventured out on his solo career. It was a brief, bittersweet experience. Once, he was approached by a well-known woman who said, "Mark, do my house. I'll tell just everybody that you've done it and you'll be famous in no time." When you're just starting out, you're hungry for that sort of talk, Mark reflects. He

RIGHT: "Patrician" decorator Mark Hampton in the foyer of his formal, yet comfortable home on New York's Park Avenue. CENTER RIGHT: On an Italian Louis XVI console in the Hampton foyer, Mark has arranged several "architectural toys", including a miniature temple by Emilio Terry. The framed picture of an interior is from *Pynes Royal Residences*, a beautiful set of hand-colored engravings from the early nineteenth-century. FAR RIGHT: On the George III secretary bookcase in the Hampton sitting room are objects made of ivory, collected by Mark's wife. The painting of the tulip is eighteenth-century French. Books are always an important element in the intelligently conceived rooms of Mark Hampton.

did the house, and waited for the publicity. The house was indeed published, but the woman claimed she had decorated it.

When he launched his Madison Avenue firm in 1976, the time was finally ripe. He'd journeyed far from the time when, after installing an air conditioner in the wall of a Fifth Avenue bedroom, he realized he had failed to ask where the outlet was. A decorator had better have a well-developed sense of humor, Mark advises, and a cooperative electrician.

Mark is known for creating comfortable environments with a pronounced architectural feel. His rooms have a

LIKES: Asher Durant paintings, Rateau bronzes, Georgian-revival period, Gothic style, seventeenth—nineteenth-century French furniture, eighteenth-century Genovese furniture, eighteenth-century Venetian furniture, plaster ceilings and mouldings, old ironwork, roof tiles, old paving stones, painted furniture, mirrors, some Art Deco furniture

DISLIKES: Cheap workmanship, glamour without comfort, 1950s and 1960s revivals, a house with no books, Jean Dubuffet paintings, new leather, modern Japanese design, plastic laminates, jacuzzis, media rooms

FAVORITE COLORS: All shades of white, Italian red, all shades of green

LEAST FAVORITE COLORS: Purple, magenta

IDEAL CLIENT: One with wonderful taste and a sense of humor who collects already and is interested in adding to his or her collection

WORST CLIENT: One with no patience

sense of both immediacy and history. He brings to his houses the traditions and craftsmanship of the past, as well as his celebrated skill at providing a deft mix of period furnishings.

The Hampton name makes frequent appearances on the International Best Dressed List, a kind of celebrity that amplifies his impeccable credentials in the highly social world in which he makes his home. He and his wife, Duane, an antiques dealer and editor, have two daughters and a very busy social life. But if Mark had his druthers, he'd be painting, writing, or digging in his garden in Southampton.

The master bedroom of the Hampton residence in New York is wallpapered in an old Chinese pattern, with a gray ground and mostly grisaille peony trees. On the bookcases, made especially to hold the red-leather-bound family albums, a constantly changing assortment of family photographs is on display. A greenish gray taffeta is used for upholstery and window treatments. Bed linens are white, covered with antique cotton lace.

NICHOLAS HASLAM
Old-school eccentric

The sameness of the world bothers Nicholas Haslam, Nicky to his friends and clients. He likes surprises. Rooms that are all of a period or all of a piece may make fine museum exhibitions, but he wouldn't want to live in them. This iconoclastic English designer cherishes the rare, be it a valuable one-of-a-kind object, a bit of thrift shop zaniness, or a unique solution to a problem. The homes that he designs are full of unexpected turns and flights of fancy.

Born in Buckinghamshire on September 27, 1939, he grew up in a sophisticated society milieu. His father was a diplomat. His mother, once the secretary of Fanny Brice, was a goddaughter of Queen Victoria. His "Aunt" Nancy was author Nancy Mitford.

As a schoolboy at Eton, Nicky decorated his rooms with leopard-spotted curtains and won every art prize the school could bestow. He attended art school after graduating from Eton, studying with Wilfred Blunt. His fine art training served him well; his clients

receive marvelous watercolor renderings of their Haslam-designed rooms.

A trip to the United States in 1961 gave focus to Nicky's considerable talents and changed his life. After working briefly at a number of jobs—with his father's small publishing company, British *Vogue*, and various newspapers—travelling about, and living in St. Tropez, he arrived in New York with photographer David Bailey and model Jean Shrimpton. He moved into and decorated an apartment near Gramercy Park, which was photographed by the *Herald Tribune*. His telephone was very busy after that, with people asking him to decorate their apartments. But he was otherwise employed, working in the art department of *Vogue*. He showed Diana Vreeland, the just-named editor, a photograph of the Beatles, still unknown in America. Vreeland recognized Nicky's nose for discovery; he stayed at *Vogue* for three years while the Beatles captured the na-

LIKES: Swedish Louis XV style, plaster, silver gilt, dainty white furniture, the city of Prague, Modern houses and furniture, elephant chintz on the backs of chairs, eighteenth-century portraits, mirrors, big tassels, old toile de Jouy, white rugs, wall sconces

DISLIKES: Orientalia, stainwood, walnut, gilding, grand Louis XIV style, narrow London houses, patterned carpets, trimmings, modern lighting, paisley, too many bed pillows, Art Deco style, Art Nouveau style, Biedermeier furniture

FAVORITE COLORS: Mauve, prune, dusty greens, black, white, pewter, oyster, swimming-pool green

LEAST FAVORITE COLORS: Orange, blue

IDEAL CLIENT: A person who doesn't have time to decorate for himself and gives his decorator not carte blanche but carte "beige"

WORST CLIENT: Those who listen to their friends, have no idea what they want, and change their mind all the time.

DREAM PROJECT: To build a wonderful palace in Barbados

LEFT: Nicholas Haslam relaxes in his London sitting room, decorated to exude the spirit of the eighteenth century.

tion's attention.

When New York began to pall, he bought a ranch in Arizona and became a cowboy, moving on to Hollywood, where he worked as a photographer. While living in America, he continued to receive design commissions in England. Finally, England claimed him. In 1972, he returned to London and devoted himself to interior decoration.

Nicky has created dreamy Edwardian rooms, but he also welcomes clients with modern houses. What he likes and does best are fantastic mixtures—distressed mirrored walls, striped glazed chintz, Louis XV chairs, and zebra skin rugs. No matter the mix, his rooms are flattering, and quirky.

While Nicky has strong opinions on the art and craft of decoration, he's the first to admit that his taste changes. He used to loathe anything Tudor; now he loves all things Tudor. For Nicky, fashion is not to be ignored.

Among things Nicholas Haslam treasures are: a fan letter he received from Nancy Lancaster, his Hampshire hideaway, and his black Pekingese. While he loves his London life, he's a gregarious man with ties on both sides of the Atlantic. Someday soon, he just may build his dream house, a palace in Barbados containing at least one rococo room.

ABOVE LEFT: Nicky's London study is wallpapered with a Tree of Life pattern, originally painted by John Fowler for Nancy Lancaster and inspired by the wall paintings of Sweden's historic Drottningholm Castle. BELOW: Silver-leaf paper covers the panels of the dining room in Nicky's flat. The wallpaper gives the impression of a mirrored surface, especially when lit by candlelight. RIGHT: A master of effects, Nicky added the "ruin" frieze, depicting brick, cracked plaster, and even spiders and cobwebs to counter the mannered wall treatment below.

LEFT: The trompe l'oeil marble walls of Nicky's bedroom are "creatively" grained above the bed, forming a ghost portrait of the decorator's Hampshire retreat. The neoclassical-style bed was designed by Haslam especially for the room. RIGHT: The luxurious bathroom in Nicky's London apartment is undeniably luxurious. Trompe l'oeil tortoiseshell walls have been painted to set off the objects perfectly.

DAVID HICKS

Establishment with a twist

David Hicks would have been more at home living in the early nineteenth century. The distinguished British designer, whose rooms at Albany in Piccadilly were once Lord Byron's, deplores the artifacts of modern life—the I.M.Pei-designed glass pyramid that houses the new entrance to the Louvre, clear lucite tissue boxes, even personal computers, which, he believes, encourage people to be even lazier than they already are. If

progress means new hybrid bicolored roses and motorcycles, he'll have none of it. His advice: put the telly on the floor under a heavy linen tablecloth and immediately go outside to work in the flower garden.

David is a passionate gardener, an authority on flowers and garden design, and the author of two books on the subjects, as well as nine on interior decoration. It is the timelessness of gardens that appeals to him. While the fashion-conscious flit from one style to another, one designer to another, redecorating a room on whim, a formal rose garden or a grove of trees will last a century.

David was born in England on March 25, 1929. His stockbroker father was devoted to his country; he made it a rule never to sleep abroad. David's education gravitated to the study of art. His decorating career was launched shortly after the end of World War II. Photographs of the Eaton Square house he did for himself were published in a leading decorating magazine. That immediately launched him as a decorator. At the time, he worked from his house, hiring a girlfriend to answer the phones—quite a different set-up than the one he operates from now. Since his well-publicized debut, he has decorated the homes of socially prominent clients on both sides of the Atlantic and designed a wide range of consumer goods—from pantyhose to luggage. David currently holds commissions in Japan for the design of major hotels in Tokyo and Kobe among others.

While David's particular taste and

RIGHT: Decorator David Hicks at home in London.

very refined style is definitively English, with his Savile Row suits, wry sense of humor and Winston Churchillesque voice, (his wife, Lady Pamela, is Lord Mountbatten's daughter), he doesn't play golf or participate in fox hunts. Unlike his father, who was uncomfortable away from his beloved country, David often goes abroad. He adores travel, starting each trip with a flower plucked from his garden. David feels English style doesn't travel as easily, however. It's too bad, he says, that the English country house is such a hot export property; the look is quite out of place in American cities.

A David Hicks house is a clean, well-lit place. His sense of rightness is grounded in the aesthetics of Euclidian geometry; his decorating style is classical in nature. He likes simplicity, strength, and clean, clear colors. He prizes sensuous fabrics, like chamois, silk, and velvet, and brilliant lacquer finishes on walls and furniture. He has always mixed the old and the new, producing crisp, uncluttered rooms that glow with quality and a vibrant mix of color. David's contribution to twentieth-century design has been considerable. His work sets trends. His experiments become "classics" that are as influential as they are beautiful.

LIKES: Chamois, lacquer walls, doors, furniture, horsehair upholstery, Russian furniture, textures (like silk velvet or heavy linen), televisions on the floor under a tablecloth

DISLIKES: Computers, amateur decorating, the English country-house look in American cities, ordinary late-nineteenth-century furniture, cut glass flower vases, gladiolas, rubber tree plants, ficus (except for lyarata), bare light bulbs, Disguised things (like boxes to hold Kleenex boxes), bright-colored front doors, cherry blossoms, motorcycles, I.M. Pei's pyramid at the Louvre, Musee d'Orsay in Paris

FAVORITE COLORS: Red, white

LEAST FAVORITE COLORS: Peacock blue and orange, especially when used together

IDEAL CLIENT: One who is sufficiently sensitive and intelligent enough to know what he doesn't want

WORST CLIENT: Indecisive

The window over the sofa in David's bedroom is
covered with a voluminous balloon shade. David is a
master of the dramatic in design.

ABOVE & LEFT: David's sitting room is bright, yet extremely sophisticated. His sense of color is unique; his taste is impeccable.

WILLIAM HODGINS

Clear and crisp

To create just the right environment for a client, it's of paramount importance that a decorator hears and understands what his client wants. All the better if the chemistry between the two is right, if there's a challenging, electric interchange of ideas. But listening is the key, and Boston-based decorator William Hodgin's strong suit.

The rooms William creates are gentle, uncontrived, perfectly scaled, and personal. He'll take pains to assemble eight unmatched chairs to surround an old French table, choosing pieces similar in style and shape, but not a set. Sets are rather dreary, he thinks, as are perfect matches. The idiosyncratic touches in his rooms, however, are never showy, never ostentatious. The garden urns and statuary he likes to use indoors add architectural accents to rooms.

William's love of lofty ceilings may be a matter of his own creature comfort. At six feet six inches tall, he needs his space. His choice of pale, neutral back-

ground colors establishes calm and clarity in his designs, bringing to the fore the treasures his rooms hold—French and Italian painted furniture, for instance, or table-top collections that make charming still-lifes in the interior landscape. He mixes old and new with sensitivity. A Hodgins house is never overfilled or overdone.

Born in Peru to Canadian parents, William spoke Spanish as a child. When he was three, the family returned to Canada, settling in London, Ontario, a sleepy university town with tall, majestic trees. Although he toyed with the idea of becoming a decorator, he attended the University of Western Ontario, first majoring in history and economics. He then set off for London and Paris, where he worked for six months in the basement of the American embassy, selling groceries.

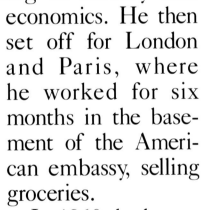

In 1960, he began his life's work in earnest, enrolling at Parsons School of Design. A five-year period working with Albert Hadley and Sister Parish completed his education; today he names them as his mentors. While he was happy in his work, he found himself unhappy in New York. Boston became his weekend escape. In 1969, he opened an office there.

An avid gardener and reader, William says he's blissfully lazy when he's not working, but he usually is—taking on new projects with enthusiasm. One New Year's Eve, he resolved to take things and people as they came and "not to make a bloody fuss about anything." This goal would allow him to achieve serenity in the face of inevitable crisis—like the day a favored client called with a question. A carpet delivery had been scheduled; the following day the furniture was to arrive. The client called when the installers unrolled the carpet. Had William ordered carpeting strewn with big purple spots, she wondered. Yes, but for his own bedroom.

When he first started out, William was doing a very small dining room with densely patterned fabric chosen for the walls and curtains, a design that employed twisted vines and leaves. He arrived at the apartment to find the wallpaper technician had hung the paper upside down. William took a deep breath and decided to do the curtains upside down. The client reports that no one has ever noticed the mistake.

William develops warm, close relationships with his clients. He'll send flowers to honor a client's birthday and receives gifts in appreciation of his work.

LEFT: William Hodgins at his Boston apartment.

LIKES: "Up" people, animals, reading, gardening

DISLIKES: Insincerity, things that look too "planned," overfilled rooms, things that match

FAVORITE COLOR: Emerald green

LEAST FAVORITE COLOR: Rust

IDEAL CLIENT: Organized and imaginative people who are good editors and can get you to think about things

WORST CLIENT: Those who do everything for show and are trying to be more than what or who they are

ABOVE: In the dining "hall" of Bill's Boston apartment, a Gothic chair shares the table with late-eighteenth-century Italian chairs, brought to the city from the decorator's Manchester County country house. The shelves are lined with creamware—Bill's favorite.

RIGHT: In the bedroom of his Manchester County house, Bill's talent for never overfilling a room is apparent. A plain canvas curtain helps to set off a French Consulate chair with just a touch of gilding. An unusual eighteenth-century cupboard stands in the corner.

ABOVE & RIGHT: Bill's own desktop is a lesson in the study of shapes. He is a master arranger—never overdoing anything.

LEFT: Faux stone walls greet the visitor in Bill's Boston home. An Italian bust takes center stage on a neoclassical console, also Italian in origin. RIGHT: The windows of Bill's Boston living room aren't dressed, so that one might always have a view of the church across the street. In front of the window: a slipper chair, a Danish sun calendar on a pedestal, a low screen, and a side table with "great feet."

NANCY HUANG

Rock-star Victorian

Manhattan-based decorator Nancy Stoddart Huang traces her Victorian roots to her paternal grandmother's house. There she lived for the first twelve years of her life—in a home where nothing had changed since her grandmother's death years before Nancy was born. From this "gingerbread pile," her father, a devotee of Modern architecture, moved the family into a one-story house with huge thermopane windows and terrazzo floors. Nancy hated it. She missed her gilt mirrors and horsehair-covered Belter loveseats. Nancy felt out of place. She has tried to get back to her roots ever since.

Antique textiles, decorative borders, eccentric wall paintings, and "grand" touches are a part of a Huang design. She creates homes that appear as if her clients inherited them—and without a tidy housekeeper! Nancy is as eccentric as the rooms she designs. While her design taste is definitively Victorian, her idea of good music is decidedly cutting edge: Rap and Heavy Metal. In fact,

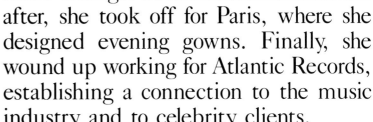

in addition to her decorating duties, she writes pop songs and manages a band.

Born in Philadelphia, Nancy attended Sarah Lawrence College. Soon after, she took off for Paris, where she designed evening gowns. Finally, she wound up working for Atlantic Records, establishing a connection to the music industry and to celebrity clients.

Nancy's years in Europe opened her eyes to the luxurious style of the nineteenth century. She visited many of the grand houses of the European elite. As a guest, Nancy stored all the decorating information away for the future: smells (Floris scents and Rigaud candles), fabrics (hand-loomed in Florence), menus and placecards (done by a calligrapher), amusing chairs (from the Giacometti studio), bath towels (as big as bed sheets), and linens (embroidered by old Italian ladies). These details are at the heart of Nancy's designs.

LIKES: Aesthetic Movement furniture, Thank-you notes, books on true crimes, shopping in London, Heavy metal and rap music, old textiles for curtains, horror movies, elaborate trim, the work of architect Julia Morgan, Stew Leonard's market in Westport, CT—especially Mrs. Leonard's meatloaf, the carrot cake, and the talking cows

DISLIKES: Antique dealers with no sense of humor, the D&D Building in New York City, celebrities with bad manners, the Right-to-Life movement, acres of "important" brown furniture, "Boomerang" tables, beanbag chairs, shag carpeting, American women who curtsy to foreign royalty, people who let small children answer their phones

FAVORITE COLORS: Grayish, faded William Morris green

LEAST FAVORITE COLOR: Hot pink

IDEAL CLIENT: Someone I'd invite over for dinner to discuss books, collecting, architecture, and decoration

WORST CLIENT: Someone who has a mate who is constantly trying to undermine a job

DREAM PROJECT: To build a house in the Gothick style, where everything revolves around one great room with fireplaces at either end

LEFT: Nancy Huang in her Manhattan apartment.

LEFT: Nancy's Egyptian-revival bedroom is elegant and luxurious. Nancy designed the sleigh bed and had hieroglyphics stenciled on the walls. The needlepoint carpet finishes the environment, which is thoroughly atmospheric—and fun to boot. BOTTOM LEFT: A section of the living room is Nancy's study. The desk, seemingly composed of old books, was made in England especially for her. On it rests some favorite classics. The wall is upholstered with a gracefully patterned Fortuny fabric. RIGHT: Nancy's sitting room is stenciled with a delicate border of fleur-de-lis. The Victorian sofa has a neo-Egyptian influence. On the wall hangs a Lucienne Commerc painting. The exotic atmosphere of the room is very high style, but Nancy has also emphasized visual and physical comfort.

JED JOHNSON

The best and the brightest

anhattan-based decorator Jed Johnson got his start in the movies. Through his friend Andy Warhol, he worked as an assistant to director Paul Morrissey on the artist's films—*Flesh, Trash, Frankenstein,* and *Dracula.* As Jed gradually learned the ins and outs of movie-making, he served as a co-director on *Bad,* another Warholian gem. The transition between filmmaking and decorating was very easy for him. When he opened his office, first out of an East Side townhouse in 1978, and later on Manhattan's West Side, he saw that creating an interior landscape was a similar task to creating the proper ambiance on-screen. Both require discipline and vision, and are concerned with the organization of elements within a "frame."

Jed's organizational skills were tested first with his decoration of Warhol's house. The artist was an intense collector of just about everything—from fine eighteenth-century furniture and Art Deco pieces to contemporary paintings, and, of course, ceramic cookie jars. Jed's intelligent and coherent handling of Warhol's collections led to other jobs, designing for many of the artist's circle of famous and powerful friends.

Jed was no fly-by-night decorator, however. In order to handle such an elite clientele, he educated himself completely in the decorative arts, becoming an expert in furniture styles, able to identify fine pieces from those that are merely good. Jed is not only a decorator, he is an advisor, whose expert eye translates a client's needs into reality—or fantasy, if they so desire.

In order to provide full-service design, Jed collaborates with architect Alan Wanzenberg. The two partners "handle" a job from start to finish, and have the ability to transform the architecture of a space readily. One must, in order to achieve the right effect, begin with a coherent, appropriate space. This is why a Jed Johnson-designed space has a certain purity. And the scale is just right.

Jed was born December 30, 1948 in Alexandria, Minnesota, but he thinks of Sacramento, California as his hometown, having lived there since the age of eight. He has a twin brother, and

LIKES: Collections, stenciling, Arts & Crafts furniture, mixing colors

IDEAL CLIENT: An involved and concerned one

WORST CLIENT: Narrow-minded, with no imagination

RIGHT: Jed Johnson in his New York duplex. A Mimmo Palladino sculpture stands on the table. In his baby picture, above, he is joined by twin brother Jay.

two older sisters and brothers. His father is in the construction business. When on a vacation in New York City, he was introduced to Andy Warhol. The rest is history, so to speak.

There is nothing superficial about Jed's work. He likes to put as many colors together in a room as possible, enjoying the richness that mixtures bring. Beautiful stenciling often brings a room together. He uses objects as centerpieces, basing the architecture and decorating scheme on a single element of historic note, or translating into reality a mood or style expressed in a particular painting, literary work, or architectural piece.

Though Jed is painstakingly precise,

he does make mistakes. He can recall ordering a sofa for an apartment in New York's Pierre Hotel that couldn't fit through the doorway. It wasn't such a catastrophe; the feet were taken off in the hall, and the sofa finally cleared the entrance. He now thoroughly measures every door and every elevator in order not to repeat this mistake. Jed prefers orderly installations. He knows his clients don't want headaches, and neither does he.

Jed adores clients who are already collectors. Whatever they own, he always tries to achieve the correct surroundings for the objects or furniture pieces.

LEFT: An assortment of telephone clocks are grouped together on Jed's library table. ABOVE, RIGHT & BELOW: Jed's sitting room contains a mosaic fireplace by Louis Millet, with mantel and surround from a Chicago home that George Maher designed, a *Mao* by Warhol, and a Palladino sculpture. The room has a nineteenth-century atmosphere.

Jed's New York library is simply decorated with a large, comfortable sofa and pillows, a graceful floor lamp, and a quiet framed landscape on the wall.

LEFT: Designing Andy Warhol's New York townhouse was Jed Johnson's first big break in the world of design. Here, the guest bedroom contains an eclectic assortment of traditional, exotic, and contemporary paintings and sculptures. The patterned wallpaper and carpeting form a vibrant background. BOTTOM LEFT: The Warhol sitting room is sedate, furnished with exquisite art deco pieces. An early Roy Lichtenstein rondel is among the collection of paintings that were on display in the Warhol residence. RIGHT: On the walls of the Warhol guest bedroom are a variety of artworks from different periods and cultures. A Jean Michel Basquiat stands in the foreground. Jed is an expert at coherently integrating art collections into spaces.

TESSA KENNEDY

East meets West

Luxurious, voluptuous rooms are London-based decorator Tessa Kennedy's trademark. She is the creator of environments that are somewhat reminiscent of Victorian period rooms, with a touch of the exotic Near East. She brings together old and new world elements skillfully. Her eye is drawn to patterns—in carpets, rugs, fabrics, and wallpapers.

Tessa blends fantasy with reality in her expert insertion of electronic gadgetry into environments that appear devoted to a less complicated way of life. She cleverly "hides" projection equipment, televisions, stereo systems, and other accoutrements of her clients' lives, many of whom are involved in the entertainment industry.

Born in Surrey on December 6, 1938, Tessa, a twin, is one of six children. Her father was a "gentleman farmer." Tessa ran away at seventeen to get married in Scotland. Her father, furious with her, got two court orders to stop Tessa, so she and her husband-to-be ran away even further—to Havana, Cuba. A scandal ensued as the story was picked up by the British press. Tessa was married, finally, in New York City. Returning to England, eventually things settled down. Tessa gave birth to three of her five children. She had never finished school, but was content to look after her children. Her husband worked as a publisher, rubbing elbows with many powerful people.

Sir James Goldsmith, aware that Tessa's husband was publishing a design book, asked him for advice on who could "do" his house. David Mlinaric was suggested. Goldsmith hired Mlinaric, who took on the job with the condition that he could work with an assistant. In stepped Tessa. She joined the Mlinaric firm.

Tessa's career was a blessing in disguise. Her marriage became "rocky," and she needed to support her children. She went after big jobs for Mlinaric, winning a competition for the redecoration of the Grosvenor House hotel. Mlinaric wasn't interested in such jobs, so Tessa felt the need to strike out on her own in 1968.

LIKES: French provincial furniture, Victorian pieces, Gothic furniture, Middle-Eastern art, Art Nouveau style, wood, inlaid mother-of-pearl, Irish furniture, Italian furniture

DISLIKES: Telephones, Robert Adam, Hepplewhite furniture, eighteenth-century French style

FAVORITE COLOR: Red

LEAST FAVORITE COLOR: Orange

IDEAL CLIENT: Someone who knows what they want and what they want to spend

WORST CLIENT: The one with no ideas or money

DREAM PROJECT: To put together a collection of fabrics and furniture designs

LEFT: Tessa Kennedy at her Manhattan pièd-a-terre.

LEFT: Provençal print pillows are comfortably arranged on the sofa of Tessa's London library. A small room, it is filled with special paintings and objects to create an even cozier feeling. BOTTOM LEFT: Family photographs and silhouettes line Tessa's desk. RIGHT: A mix of Byzantine and Gothic elements contribute to the design for Tessa's own bedroom. She has an unusual sense of style and is known for her bold pattern-on-pattern combinations.

DAVID KLEINBERG

Preferred by royalty

Some people say David Kleinberg is to decorating what Ralph Lauren is to fashion. David skillfully adapts the classic looks, making them seem fresh and appropriate for today's more complicated life-styles. Certainly, working for the prestigious Parish-Hadley firm in New York for the past seven years has made David realize that he is part of a great tradition of American decorating. He is proud of that connection, and through it has learned a great deal about the subtleties of fine design. David has absorbed both Sister Parish's acute sense of what correct American-style English decorating is all about and Albert Hadley's finely tuned academic approach to design.

David's own rooms have a unique sense of style. As with the slightly old-fashioned bias to the cut of his own clothes, David favors traditional design. Though a master of "retrospective" interiors, David's rooms glimmer, revealing the bit of fun he has in putting a scheme together. His rooms are fresh and a bit frisky—never dowdy. They are clean—not just tidy, but squeaky clean. The decor is studied, but relaxed; a bit formal, but always gracious.

David is rather doted upon by his clients, who find him lively and intelligent to deal with. And his rooms strike one the same way. The Greenwich, Connecticut home he and Sister Parish designed for polo enthusiast Henryk de Kwiatkowski so struck the visiting Duchess of York that, rather controversially, she decided the Parish-Hadley look was for her. The duchess hired the American firm to decorate her English home, though eventually she hired, more appropriately, a British designer. But for a brief moment, the decorating world was abuzz with the joyous notion that American decorating had eclipsed its more heavily tradition-bound and celebrated counterpart across the Atlantic.

David was born on July 23, 1954 in Brooklyn and raised in Great Neck, New York, an affluent Long Island suburb. His father owns a domestic security systems business and his mother is an elementary school teacher. He grew up with his older broth-

...younger sister in a house decorated in a manner almost alien to the approach he now employs. His parents furnished the family home with now-classic Modern pieces, ranging from George Nelson and Charles Eames pieces for Herman Miller to Eero Saarinen's Knoll-produced designs. Friends who knew him then say there wasn't one bit of chintz in the whole house!

After attending Trinity College in Hartford, Connecticut for four years as a liberal arts major (David chose the school because he could have both a car and a dog there), he spent six months in Rome, soaking up the classic Italian culture and cuisine (David, to this day, appreciates fine cuisine, as well as a beautifully designed kitchen—he doesn't like to cook, however). Returning to New York, he worked a summer for the renowned Manhattan decorators Denning and Fourcade, and spent five "educational" years with prominent residential interior designer Mara Palmer. His learning process proved quite successful. He took his portfolio to Parish-Hadley, who were astonished with this young man's distinguished work and sense of style. When Parish-Hadley hired him, he was named a junior member of the team—not an assistant, as is usually their policy with new employees.

LIKES: Quality furniture, thank-you notes, ballet, Chinese food, Neogothic-revival furniture, the "chase"

DISLIKES: Opera, reproductions, fabrics with designs larger than his own head, country music, Staffordshire figures

FAVORITE COLORS: Beige, ivory, brown, blue-green

LEAST FAVORITE COLORS: Purple, hot orange, blue

IDEAL CLIENT: A person with instinct, knowledge, faith, enthusiasm, and a good budget

WORST CLIENT: An insecure person who doesn't trust himself

DREAM PROJECT: To design sets for the ballet

BELOW: David Kleinberg at home on Manhattan's Upper East Side.

LEFT: An "interesting" Italian mirror hangs above the Biedermeier secretary in David's Manhattan sitting room. The vase on display was found in a junk shop on Long Island several years ago. ABOVE: Another view of David's tasteful sitting room. In front of the damask-upholstered mahogany screen is a standing lamp, made from a Regency pole screen that once belonged to a client. RIGHT: A bust of Sir Walter Scott surveys David's sitting room. The blue glass ball on display was a gift from Albert Hadley. FAR RIGHT: David has a special talent for arranging objects. Many of the things placed throughout his Manhattan apartment have a special meaning to him. The small dog figure on the table was purchased by David when he was a boy.

A. MICHAEL KRIEGER
Discipline and dash

Rooms designed by A. Michael Krieger speak of comfort, yet are characterized by an often whimsically eclectic, but restrained visual sensibility. Michael's choices of furnishings and color schemes reflect his preference for the classics over trendy intrusions that have little to do with the way people live.

If Michael has a trademark or signature, it is his use of "found objects." In his own apartment, the decorator has incorporated large industrial bolts found  during the reconstruction of New York's Queensborough Bridge, an "ancient" air-conditioning grate, and a discarded truck shock absorber that looks like an oversized corkscrew. He places these industrial discoveries among objects and furnishings of more obvious decorative value for a wonderful juxtaposition of surfaces, shapes, and textures.

Michael attempts to expand his client's notions of what can be attractive to live with, beyond the usual nineteenth-century knick-nacks and the botanical prints he sees as decorating "stereotypes." He challenges the hierarchy of good taste in decorating, creating a new

appreciation for a beautiful object, whatever its provenance. Though "not everyone wants to live with old bolts," he adds.

Michael was born in Ossining, New York on May 5, 1955. He grew up in Connecticut. His father was a publisher and a medical journalist. He describes his mother as "a very independent woman" who was always interested in design and created a home for her family in a very old barn, prefiguring the conver-

RIGHT: Decorator Michael Krieger at his Manhattan apartment.

sion mania of later decades. Michael attended Cornell University, where he took courses in theatrical set design and filmmaking, as well as art and architectural history.

After graduation, he worked at an advertising agency and as a graphic designer, but was rather uninspired. He was more interested in sculpture, creating "assemblages" of junk in his spare time. An architect friend, seeing his talent in putting things together, asked him to decorate his house. With this first assignment Michael realized that interior design utilized his skills in assemblage.

Through family connections, Michael was introduced to New York deco-

LIKES: Italian furniture, Delft china, handmade fabrics, French furniture, white walls, sisal flooring, metal furniture, early Spanish Baroque architecture, Flemish still-life paintings, rooms with tall ceilings, rattan furniture, antiquities, simple curtains, Cy Twombly paintings, anything by Giacometti

DISLIKES: Shag carpeting, Austrian shades, satin in most colors, anything made of lucite

FAVORITE COLORS: Blue, neutrals

IDEAL CLIENT: One who is receptive to new ideas and has a passion about something—a house, an art collection

WORST CLIENT: A rigid thinker

DREAM PROJECT: To restore a period house

rator Kevin McNamara, who gave Michael his first break. Later, he worked as an assistant to decorator Mark Hampton and then to Mel Dwork. In the mid-1970s Angelo Donghia, the then-reigning "king" of interior design, hired Michael. Having apprenticed with some of the greatest names in design, he decided to strike out on his own, running a successful independent firm for three years. The Donghia firm, after Angelo's death in 1985, asked him back to supervise the residential division of the company. He held that position for two years before returning to private practice. Michael's career has been rich and varied in experience.

LEFT: For a model apartment in New York, Michael created a thoroughly modern environment. All the details in the space refer to the work of furniture master Diego Giacometti. Even the Krieger-designed console covering the unsightly radiator carries a Giacometti-inspired pattern. RIGHT: The seating area of the model apartment is furnished with a Schiaparelli-designed curved sofa, a Donghia "throne" chair, a Giacometti lamp, and a round table of Michael's design. The room is unmistakenly contemporary, yet is reminiscent of high-style 1940s interiors.

LEFT: This room, for a Southampton, New York show house, features painted pelmets above the windows, inspired by curtains Michael saw in an early-eighteenth-century American painting, a Krieger-designed table with column legs, and a pair of Giacometti chairs (one is authentic; the other a reproduction). BELOW: Michael's Manhattan bedroom is furnished with a bed he found at a New York antique shop. The bed has a notable history: it was brought back from Europe in the forties by Eleanor Brown of McMillen as an example of French design of the time. The screen behind the bed is Michael's own design. A beautiful eighteenth-century hall chair stands in front of the window. Objects and artifacts are displayed on tall pedestals that embellish the architectural quality of the space. RIGHT: Krieger is known for his appreciation of industrial artifacts, often mixing them with "fine" objects.

MICHAEL LA ROCCA

Refined luxury

The consummate professional, Michael La Rocca is the creator of environments that are as inviting as they are spectacular. He strives to "ameliorate the quality of life" of his clients. He tells a story about one couple who lived in a huge apartment for years. They never entertained. After Michael had completed the decoration of their apartment, he was invited to the first of many dinner parties they threw. This quiet couple became wonderful entertainers. Michael is proud that he, in some way, could affect this couple's life. After creating a home for them, his clients took the cue.

Michael's rooms have strong presence. He is not afraid of a bit of glitz here and there to spark up some excitement. He's also not afraid of white walls. A contemporary frame around a room of period furnishings offers a fresh look, he believes.

Born in New York City on March 24, 1938, Michael had what he calls "a very nice childhood." His parents, second-generation Americans, encouraged Michael when he showed promise in music. He studied piano and voice, though eventually deciding to attend Brooklyn's Pratt Insti-

tute, entering their four-year interior design program. Upon graduation, he decided to work for an architectural firm, though after a while he got bored with that, joining the army. When he'd fulfilled his service obligations, he found employment with an industrial design firm involved in work for the World's Fair in Seattle. Still in his early twenties, he joined a commercial design firm next, ending his "apprentice" years with an eight-year stint in the office of designer David Whitcomb. From 1970 to 1983, he went into partnership with David Anthony Easton. The two decorators parted ways to pursue solo careers.

Though one wouldn't think decorators of such stature make mistakes, they do. Michael once designed a "very good-looking sofa" for a client. He had it made. Disaster! The sofa couldn't fit in the elevator of the apartment building. It couldn't fit through a window. The truckers had to carry this "big white elephant" up eighteen floors. "Those truckers never forgave me for that," he says.

LIKES: Music, playing the piano, theater, gardening, natural light in a room, Biedermeier furniture, Empire style

DISLIKES: Victorian rooms, trendiness

FAVORITE COLORS: Coral, Venetian red, ivory, sienna, ochre

LEAST FAVORITE COLORS: Purple, orange, mustard

IDEAL CLIENT: An enthusiastic one

WORST CLIENT: A financially petty and self-centered one

LEFT: Michael La Rocca at his New York apartment.

The dining room of a Greenwich, Connecticut house was given Michael's signature—opulence and appropriate reserve.

RIGHT: For a Greenwich, Connecticut client, Michael worked with a collection of fine eighteenth- and nineteenth-century French country furniture to create an impressive and comfortable environment.

ABOVE: The entrance to Michael's high-rise apartment in New York. The decorator has transformed a boxy, rather standard interior into a grand, comfortable statement.

LEFT: For a New York fashion designer's townhouse, Michael used a "draped fabric" wallpaper for a theatrical effect in the entrance foyer.

RIGHT: Cabinets, designed by Michael for the living/dining room of a New York townhouse, have the feeling of Biedermeier pieces crossed with 1940s French furniture designs. The whole room has the character of a nineteenth-century space.

ANN LE CONEY

More is never enough

New York decorator Ann Le Coney likes a room to be lively and interesting. Her version of English-style decorating is at odds with the Mies van der Rohe axiom "less is more." In fact, she shares a philosophy more akin to American architect Robert Venturi, who says "less is a bore." Ann's rooms are far from boring. They are filled with objects, furniture, paintings, and a symphony of patterns and colors. When Ann puts together a collection of items, it doesn't mean a dozen, or even two dozen, of something. Her taste borders on the excessive, tempered with a certain harmony. There is a consistency to what some might deem the madness of her schemes. The most appropriate comment to make upon entering a Le Coney-designed space is, "Why not?"

Ann was born in Rumson, New Jersey on July 27, 1946. Her father was a businessman. After attending college in Washington, D.C., her first job was with Chemical Bank in New York City. At twenty-four, she married, decorating her own house. Her friends thought she had the right touch and urged her to train with a "big decorator." She managed to work as an assis-

tant to Mario Buatta, moving on to a stint as an assistant to decorator Melanie Chen, and then to a position as Betty Sherrill's assistant at McMillen.

Ann learned a lot about quality decorating through her two years with Sherrill. At one point, when she was decorating a house for an old friend, she decided to order a sofa that was bought for its price rather than its quality. She thought she'd save her client-friend a bit of money. The sofa was a disaster, and her friend stopped speaking to her. Ann learned the lesson that "you get what you pay for." This decorator has never scrimped since, and her choices in furnishings are never a compromise.

Ann's particular look demands quality detail. Every item in her rooms is a carefully selected gem. Each silver bowl, every Staffordshire dog figure, and each architectural drawing must be able to stand alone. Without this passionate quest for the best, the LeConey style wouldn't have the same spirit.

> **LIKES:** Needlepoint cushions and carpets, Staffordshire dogs, chintz, silver frames
>
> **DISLIKES:** Plants, stage-set interiors, the "contemporary" look
>
> **FAVORITE COLOR:** Dark green
>
> **LEAST FAVORITE COLORS:** Peach, brown, orange
>
> **IDEAL CLIENT:** The person who is totally sympathetic to your way of thinking
>
> **WORST CLIENT:** Someone who thinks he knows more than you do
>
> **DREAM PROJECT:** A big job in Europe

RIGHT: Ann LeConey in her New York apartment.

LEFT: A collection of blue-and-white porcelain plates is displayed on the walls of Ann's living room. Beautiful chintzes cover the sofa and chair. Staffordshire dogs, another of Ann's collections, can be seen on the coffee table.

LEFT: Ann used chintz fabric on the walls of her bedroom for a softer look. CENTER LEFT: The floor and walls of Ann's foyer are handpainted in a stone pattern. Curtains sweep down to the floor. The window treatment is very much a part of Ann's "layered look." BOTTOM LEFT: There is a richness to the decor of Ann's living room. Pictures line the walls, which are painted with watercolors—not glazed.

DANIELA LEUSCH
Italian style

There is a gracious atmosphere in every room that Daniela Leusch creates. As a parent and a frequent hostess, she knows how a house or apartment is lived in, what works and what does not. She has a special eye for detail, knowing that the way a picture is framed, a bed is made, a table is set, and a drawing room is arranged are important and noticed aspects of a design scheme. Special touches abound.

Daniela was born in Milan on June 9, 1947. Her father, of Belgian origin, was a businessman for Black & Decker. Her mother is Italian through and through. She and her brother attended German-run schools in Milan. Daniela went on to study at the Goethe Institute in Munich. She was married at a relatively young age, divorced, and married again. Together, she and her second husband designed a line of children's bathing suits. The marriage didn't last, however, and Daniela needed to work in order to support her two children. Always known for her good taste and excellent sense of design, Daniela decided to become a dec-

orator. Her first job was decorating the house of Italian socialite Anna Pagliari in the south of France. Her design for the villa, decorated in Arabian style, caught the eye of the directors of the CIGA hotel chain, which owned some of the finest properties in Italy. Daniela was asked to redo the rooms for their hotels in Rome, Venice, Florence, and Milan—a very large job.

Her first mistake involved the deco-

RIGHT: Daniela Leusch at her apartment in the heart of Milan.

ration of a bedroom in Milan for the woman who represented the Chanel fashion empire in Italy. A large beam cut off the room, making the ceiling very low. Daniela asked the workmen to remove the beam. The next day, the contractors phoned her with the bad news: the roof was starting to fall in. It was winter, and snow was predicted. While everyone was afraid of the roof caving in, the workmen managed to reinforce the roof, still allowing Daniela to "open up" the space. She is forever worried that, in her desire to "improve" a space, she may again go overboard.

Another mishap occurred when Dan-

iela was decorating the apartment of a Milanese industrialist. Only one detail remained incomplete—the upholstery on the dining room chairs. Daniela had the chairs removed and taken to the upholsterer, without realizing that the client was planning a formal dinner party the same evening. While the man was changing into black tie, the butler inquired as to the whereabouts of the dining chairs. There was enormous confusion as guests arrived. The client and his staff were convinced there had been a robbery. He phoned the concierge, who explained that Daniela had popped in during the day. "The poor man had to change his plans completely," says Daniela, "he had to take everyone out to a restaurant for the evening." The dining room chairs, naturally, turned out beautifully.

Daniela is a knowledgeable, precise and ultimately practical professional. She has a legion of craftsmen whom she trusts to make napery, curtains, frames, and upholstery to meet her exacting standards.

LEFT: The details of Daniela's Milan dining room contribute to its overall sophistication. Daniela is especially adept at framing pictures in a special way. Here, six engravings are grouped together within a single frame for a grand effect. RIGHT: The hallway, painted in faux stone, has a warm feeling. The Roman busts on the console add a neoclassical touch. BOTTOM RIGHT: Daniela's sitting room offers plenty of seating. The warm, faux stone walls are seen throughout the apartment.

BRIAN MCCARTHY

On the way up

To excel as a decorator, a person needs not only a good eye and familiarity with furniture and fabric styles, but also on-the-job training—from professionals who are well versed in the tricks of the trade, so to speak. Young decorator Brian Mc-Carthy of New York has had the good fortune to start his career in one of the best places for the development of professionals in the field: Parish-Hadley Associates.

Born in Washington, D.C. on September 1, 1960, Brian grew up in Bethesda, Maryland. He attended Pratt Institute in Brooklyn, spending a semester of his time there studying in Copenhagen. Graduating in 1982, Brian embarked on a freelance design career. A year later, he was hired as an assistant to Albert Hadley. Under Hadley's tutelage, Brian quickly learned about the world of high-style interior design.

Brian's approach is clearly influenced by Hadley's methods. He takes his time in "forming" the proper aesthetic: "If I'm too quick, nothing fits in quite the right way." Brian pays a great deal of attention to the details of a job: "Simple solutions are often the most difficult to find."

Brian has developed his own signature as well. What characterizes his emerging style is his particular take on the classic English-style interiors that have made Parish-Hadley an American force to be reckoned with. His rooms have a more "Continental," European-style flair.

The decorating business is a people

LEFT: Brian McCarthy at home. RIGHT: Brian's country house living room is furnished with a plush sofa and a seventeenth-century tea table, among other beautiful things. FAR RIGHT: The dining room's Brazilian mahogany Empire sideboard is from Brian's grandmother's house.

business, in Brian's eyes. Though he likes to maintain an objective, professional persona with clients, he often cannot help getting involved in their lives. "When you have to do a person's closets, you often find the most interesting things," he says, "like wigs, black leather masks, and you really get to know the people you are working for."

As an example of his clients' eccentricity, Brian cites the time workmen were installing a big black bathtub in an apartment bathroom. While placing a mirror on the wall above the tub they accidentally scratched its porcelain surface. The client, wearing one blue sock and one yellow sock (for

whatever reason), went berserk. He got too close to the edge of the tub and fell into it, getting soaked (the tub was filled with water to test for leaks). Prior to the installation, this same client had arrived in the plumbing fixture showroom to "try out" the bathroom. Dressed in a bathing suit and carrying his own towel, the client jumped in, then complained about the water in the tub being too cold. Though clients keep Brian on his toes, he's learned to accept their idiosyncrasies with a grin as he works to create their homes. His future looks very bright—and Parish-Hadley can count on him to take the firm into the next century.

ROBERT METZGER

All that glitters

Glamour is an integral part of Robert Metzger's approach to design. He loves drama, opulence, and things that make a clear statement. He isn't afraid of colors, and bold flourishes are his trademark. A house has to be "outstanding," he says, and that means every detail has to be right—down to the proper linens. A Metzger design is not wishy-washy or subject to fashion and decorating fads.

Robert is an avid shopper. He  searches passionately for just the right pieces to make a room come together. He is always on the go, checking with antique dealers when new shipments come in, haunting showrooms in the never-ending search for the right stuff, even browsing around in antique shops on his summer weekend retreats to Long Island.

Robert "darling" was born in Manhattan on October 1, 1939. He jokes, "Thank God my father was born before me," as his father was in the meat and poultry business, so the family couldn't possibly starve. Robert attended New York University, graduating with a degree in Business Administration in 1961. He didn't want to go into the family business, so the most glamorous possibility was a job on Wall Street. He became an investment analyst. After two years, and with a hefty bonus, he left the financial world, traveling to Europe for five months.

When he arrived back in his hometown, Robert enrolled in the New York School of Interior Design. Upon graduation from that institution, he started working for an antique shop called "Past and Present." He stayed there eight

RIGHT: Decorator Robert Metzger at his Manhattan apartment. His signed desk by Kemp is at the right.

years, doing everything from window displays to bookkeeping. A customer of the store asked him to decorate his house one day. So began Robert's successful career. He has never worked for a big design firm and says he never will. Operating his own firm at first was "like shooting craps in Las Vegas," he quips. The first time he ordered a sofa for a client, he couldn't sleep the whole night. When putting rooms together, he depended on his gut reactions. Given his success, "they must be pretty good," he says with a laugh.

Robert's clients come to trust him implicitly. One client, who had recently undergone a face-lift operation, went to survey the job the Metzger office was doing. When she arrived at the apartment, the workmen were painting the ceiling of the sitting room. She looked up (with difficulty, as she couldn't move her head too much, and her eyes even less) and screamed, hating the color. She immediately phoned Robert. He couldn't sleep because of her tirade. The next day, Robert found out that the woman had seen the primer color being applied to the room's ceiling. Such are the downs and ups of a decorator's life.

Though Robert is the consummate decorator, don't expect to see him in his autumn years still running through his mecca, New York City's Decoration and Design Building (the D&D, to those in the know). Robert wants to transcend the design world, becoming rich *and* famous—a household name, like Brillo!

Robert Metzger has worked in association with Michael Christiano for thirteen years. Christiano, who shares Robert's demanding aesthetic, is a graduate of the architecture school at the University of Virginia. The two have many important clients across the country.

LIKES: Shagreen boxes and objects, Regency period gilt furniture, penwork on ivory, Louis XVI furniture, Charles X furniture, Biedermeier furniture, inlaid marble, shopping—but not for food or in department stores

DISLIKES: Victorian style, French pleats and double welting, "floosy" fabrics, to walk into a room and know who did it, Tiffany glass, Art Nouveau glass, the same scheme twice

FAVORITE COLORS: Jade green, beige, taupe, red, blue, peach, mauve, sherbet colors

LEAST FAVORITE COLORS: Orange, leaf green, hot pink, Memphis colors

IDEAL CLIENT: A woman with a past and a man with a future

WORST CLIENT: The one who doesn't know what he wants and cannot pay his bills

DREAM PROJECT: To make his name a household word, like Brillo

Like banners, these festive kites parade across the unpainted ceiling tins covering Robert's bedroom wall. An assortment of canes, and a tulip-filled vase add to the "holiday" spirit. Robert designed the parchment and ivory bed.

Robert collects Japanese bronze and ivory animal figures. Stored in miniature showcases, these artifacts are displayed on the bold, reflective surface of a mirrored art deco backgammon table.

JUAN PABLO MOLYNEUX
Grand and glamorous

With clients spread across two continents, Juan Pablo Molyneux is an international frequent flyer. In fact, he would love to learn to pilot a plane, as it would satisfy his love of speed and drama as well as his need to jet from here to there.

Born in Santiago, Chile, on November 4, 1947, Juan Pablo and his older brother grew up in a wealthy family that traces its roots to England. Juan Pablo was sent off to The Grange, an English boarding school in Santiago, a "finishing school" in England, and ended up in France, happily unemployed. Alarmed by their son's aimlessness, the family summoned Juan Pablo back to Santiago, where he enrolled in architecture school. Student life was lovely; Juan Pablo was in no hurry to see it end. He spent some time at the Beaux Arts in Paris, studied archaeology, and finally earned his architecture degree in Chile.

Juan Pablo began his career with a construction firm, designing and building houses and highways. He turned to furniture design, creating neoclassical revival pieces that were sold throughout South America. He and his wife Pilar, whom he married in 1976, decided to head for London, stopping first in Buenos Aires. The "stop" lasted twelve years. Juan Pablo opened a decorating studio. The city embraced him, captivated by his classic European style.

Juan Pablo smiles and flinches when recalling his worst decorating nightmare. In Buenos Aires, he hurried through the raw space that was the new apartment of a rich, very busy woman. Always in a rush, his client quickly surveyed the plans that Juan Pablo drew up and nodded. Do the work, she told him, and call when the apartment's finished. He did, and took his client through the elegant, just-completed rooms. She praised his work, admiring everything, but told him that unfortunately the apartment was not hers. He learned the value of getting to know both his clients and their addresses well.

In 1983, Juan Pablo opened shop in New York. While he now lives and works in New York, he continues to serve his Argentinian clients, who wouldn't make a move without him.

RIGHT: Juan Pablo Molyneux before a seventh-century mythological tapestry in his Manhattan sitting room.

LIKES: Aston Martin automobiles, dogs, storms, Fortuny fabrics, knobs, tools, nails, and screws, taffeta, velvet, Gothic period

DISLIKES: Taxis, chintz, gossip, flashy decor

FAVORITE COLORS: Red, yellow, black, taupe

LEAST FAVORITE COLORS: Calypso orange, mustard, fuschia, emerald green

IDEAL CLIENT: One who could be described as cultivated

WORST CLIENT: An ignorant, nouveau riche person who thinks he knows everything

ABOVE: With imaginative innovation, Juan Pablo has set off the marble fireplace in his sitting room with a mirrored wall. The room is filled with framed and reflected images. LEFT: This large, wood-paneled library offers a retreat for even the most restless of readers. Two solid-colored, cushioned sofas face one another on either side of a fireplace, room for an intimate group.

LEFT: Lucite columns designed by Juan Pablo give his bedroom an ethereal and contemporary feel that is countered by a more earthy seventeenth-century portrait.

RIGHT: A carousel horse in the Molyneux library adds a playful note.

RENZO MONGIARDINO

The maestro of Milan

Renzo Mongiardino tells this story: A long time ago, a Greek philosopher strolled with his student through a cypress grove, talking of beauty. The student asked if the Parthenon was beautiful. Yes, the philosopher replied, because one feels it has been there forever. This is Renzo's idea of beauty.

The ultimate compliment you can pay the distinguished Milanese architect is that his designs embody the quality of timelessness. He believes that interiors should appear ordained and thoroughly natural. Nothing should scream, "Look at me!" While his clients come to him with possessions that might be snapped up by museums—seventeenth-century Roman cabinets, rare Japanese screens, Etruscan cups—the rooms that he creates with them are always harmonious and comfortable. "Museums are a little bit like cemeteries," Renzo says.

Born May 12, 1916 in Genoa, Renzo has always lived in a beautiful, old house. His father was an engineer, a man of strong opinions; his mother displayed a rich sensibility for decoration, favoring cashmere and intricate paisleys. As an architecture student at the polytechnic in Milan, he began working for some of his professors; by the age of 25, he went into business for himself. His primary interest has always been architecture. His interest in decoration was somewhat of an afterthought, a natural consequence of the fact that he always likes to finish what he starts.

For Renzo, antiquities are the future as well as the past. After all, he reasons, we live the same life that people lived 200 years ago. The human condition does not really change. There is always love, jealousy, marriage, and home. He adores massive pieces of furniture of many periods: Italian and French Renaissance, Baroque, Gothic. The comfort and practical sense of late-nineteenth-century English houses delight him. Charles Rennie Mackintosh chairs are anathema, an imposition on the interior landscape; the

LIKES: Very large pieces of furniture, Baroque style, Napoleon III period, antique fabrics, Liberty prints (sometimes), Italian and French Renaissance furniture, late-nineteenth-century English style

DISLIKES: Small, fragile tables, Art Deco furniture, any reminders of the Fascist period, rooms that look like museum displays, paintings without lights on them, ostentation

FAVORITE COLOR: Red

LEAST FAVORITE COLORS: Acid hues, like orange-lemon

IDEAL CLIENT: One with a clear idea of what they want

WORST CLIENT: Those who collect clippings from House & Garden or The World of Interiors and say, "do this."

DREAM PROJECT: To write about architecture, decoration, and ideas

RIGHT: Renzo Mongiardino at his desk in his Milan apartment.

A rich border design painted by Renzo. In his apartment studio, Renzo is always looking for new ways of embellishing his room design.

madly idiosyncratic furniture of the Italian Memphis collection has its place, a child's bedroom. Renzo's passion for old, magisterial furnishings extends to the bedroom, where he feels antique pieces, with their warmth and heart, work better than new ones do.

A consummate creator of atmosphere, Renzo steeps himself in the personality of his clients and observes the atmosphere and the architecture of their apartments and houses. Some are at first unnerved as they watch him surveying their rooms, scratching his beard and lost in thought. For each commission, he carefully considers what he calls the "music of colors," the rapport one color has when set next to another. For a London library, with its misty light, he will choose a strong color, one of his favorite reds; in Palermo, with its blazing sun, he may work with an all-white scheme.

Renzo observes that dining rooms lead a strange life. They must work for two as well as

twelve. He might solve the problem by using two square marble-topped tables set on fluted, petrified wood pedestals. He is especially attuned to decorating hallways, entryways, and passages— spaces that have a pronounced architectural character. The small rooms he decorates are very full, while classically proportioned grand spaces are kept free of excess decoration.

As a designer for the theater, movies, and opera, Renzo is a master of illusion. He has worked closely with Italian director Franco Zeffirelli on films and Covent Garden productions, projects Renzo finds exhilarating but exhausting. Renzo has designed the settings for *Tosca* in London, *Don Pasquale* in Milan, and for a production of *The Taming of the Shrew*, starring Elizabeth Taylor and Richard Burton. Today he spends most of his time working with two assistants in his tiny studio in Milan. A loose confederation of his students, who live in Rome, London, Paris and New York, work with him on his many international commissions. His work spills over into his apartment with fabrics, renderings, and bits of marble cluttering his bedside table—even the elegant salon, with its patchwork curtains that once framed the windows in his grandmother's house.

LEFT: A cluttered corner of Renzo's studio where he "stashes" objects, clippings, fabric samples, and other "things" that once inspired him. RIGHT: Renzo paints in the tradition of the old masters. Here, an assortment of his pigments, brushes, and other supplies at his home/office in Milan.

Book-filled shelves behind glass cabinet doors line this spacious, sitting room. A large sofa with patterned cushions, a hanging lamp, a globe on a wooden base, and decorative detailing along the ceiling give the room a majestic quality.

Roland Barthes ❧ Erté ❧ F.M.Ricci

ABOVE: The bedroom is filled with artwork. One wall is lined with paintings, photographs, and a sculpture: all portraying different images of women. The patterns of the wallpaper and upholstery show Renzo's love of the nineteenth century. RIGHT: A portrait bust and porcelain swan, as well as an assortment of paintings give the bedroom a traditional look. More abstract touches are added by the lamps and vase. The Empire sleigh bed has fabric draped over it from the back wall to make it appear "whole."

JUAN MONTOYA

Strong and bold

Once an astute creator of minimalist, high-tech interiors, Juan Montoya's decorating style has shifted, embracing the past he once shunned. Instead of stark, thoroughly contemporary environments, the New York-based decorator puts together rooms that are a reflection of today's more relaxed attitudes. Past and present are dramatically paired.

Juan's rooms have a contemporary, architectural feeling. They are appreci-

ated for their warmth, refinement, and tailoring. Selective in his purchases for clients, he puts together Art Deco pieces and antiques. The Montoya look is a wonderful mix of textures and materials, crisply presented in an envelope that is often architecturally dramatic. No fuss. No clutter. Very comfortable.

Juan was born in Bogota, Colombia

on May 7, 1945. His father was a diplomat, representing Colombia in various countries throughout South America. Juan was tutored privately in painting throughout his childhood. At eighteen, he chose to attend the Parsons School of Design in New York, studying painting and eventually graduating with a degree in environmental design in 1972. Upon graduation, he moved to Paris, working as a freelance designer there, then on to Milan where he took on a number of design jobs, even designing furniture (for which he is known today). He returned to New York, working for a company that created the "total" design of houses in the Caribbean. He then worked for an office design firm, eventually opening his own office in 1976.

Architecture is an important part of Juan's work. He sees the interior structure as a base from which to decorate, as the proper architectural envelope can change the character of a space. Lighting also plays a special role in setting the proper mood.

The completed projects in Juan's portfolio are varied. While houses and apartments are his primary focus, about thirty percent of his work each year is in the commercial design arena. He has designed the inte-

LIKES: Art Deco furniture, African art, Venetian masks, Rococo style, Venetian palazzi, the English countryside, Scotland, summer, the mountains of Colombia, tailored clothes, good lighting, tweedy fabrics, stripes, printed and chintz fabrics, painted furniture, silk, cashmere, Italian islands

DISLIKES: Track lighting, the sound of the telephone, 1940s and 1950s furniture, little objects and clutter, winter, polyester, canopy beds

FAVORITE COLORS: Butterscotch, forest green, vanilla

IDEAL CLIENT: Has a definite opinion

WORST CLIENT: Cannot make up his mind

DREAM PROJECT: To design a cathedral, a glamorous restaurant, a house on a desert island, and a yacht

riors of private planes, offices for the clothing store Barneys New York, showrooms for Christian Dior, Jones New York boutiques, and numerous furniture showrooms and shops. Clients come to Juan for his brilliant interpretations of their life- or business-style. His clients, ideally, have a strong sense of self and are not afraid to take chances. They are comfortable with the idea that Juan's talent lies in his ability to create a "new" environment that, while incorporating pieces from the past, is a fresh and uncompromisingly current statement, dependent not on fashionable tastes or trends, but on what feels right.

LEFT: Decorator Juan Montoya. RIGHT: This Montoya-designed hallway is luminous with an array of reflections. On a cobalt blue glass wall hangs a Venetian mirror, next to which is reflected a Jean Michel Basquiat painting. High-tech bands of lights are set into the tops of the lacquered doorway columns.

RIGHT: The assertive, geometric rhythms in this Kips Bay show house room are created with art deco furniture, African objects, and a Montoya armoir and pedestal. BELOW: This sunny library combines Montoya's bold architectural detailing with period pieces. A bronze Bacchus is surrounded by turn-of-the-century Viennese clock chairs. The table is covered with an English turn-of-the-century throw. A Chinese bronze pot from the early seventeenth century has been made into a planter. Modern accents include the leather chairs, upholstered with cushion ticking, and rubbed ash shelves.

ABOVE: Juan's bedroom is decorated with simple forms from different cultures, such as this Japanese ceremonial chest and a collection of nineteenth-century French pottery. A cylindrical iron bedpost creates an interesting juxtaposition with the wooden ceiling beams. The door is a Montoya design. LEFT: The light-filled kitchen is furnished with Adirondacks furniture and French pottery.

ABOVE: The Montoya dining room, with a bamboo-covered ceiling and granite floor and fireplace, offers a bold combination of materials. Furnished with objects collected over the years, it is decorated with an eighteenth-century chapel bench from the south of France, an oak refectory table, early American chairs, and Moroccan and African vessels. The "server" is a Montoya design of oak and iron.

SANDRA NUNNERLEY

New international style

International-style design is often viewed as the antithesis of warmth and coziness. In Manhattan-based decorator Sandra Nunnerley's mind, a room can successfully include elements and details from the past and present to provide a comfortable and relaxed environment geared to the lifestyle of a contemporary person. While International-style interiors allow little or no decoration, Sandra's version of the style adapts to the needs of the individual and, while presenting a clean aesthetic, is punctuated with furnishings, fabrics, works of art, and objects from a variety of sources. She tailors a room to a client, always paying attention to the "shell" before proceeding. "If the 'bones' are there, then everything is possible," she says.

Sandra was born on January 11, 1954 in Wellington, New Zealand. Her father was a lawyer; her mother, a journalist. She attended college in Sydney, Australia, studying art, architecture, and design. Right after graduation, she worked in a Sydney art gallery for a while. Toward the end of the 1970s, Sandra decided to leave the land down-under, to travel and explore the rest of the world. After living in London,

among many other places, she was drawn to New York, taking a job at a Soho art gallery. Her career in design happened entirely by accident. An Australian friend hired Sandra and an architect to work on his apartment in New York. The apartment turned out fabulously. With her first taste of decorating success, she went to work in the residential design division of a large corporate design firm. Soon after, she went solo. Though trained in architecture, Sandra does rely on her art background a great deal. She cites it as instrumental in establishing her sense of color and perspective.

One of Sandra's first mistakes was to order a sofa for a client that couldn't fit in the apartment building's freight elevator. Sandra "brilliantly" had the idea of cutting the sofa in half, right in the lobby. She had it sawed in two, called the reupholsterer for a "quickie" repair, and no one ever suspected a thing. To this day, she is always wary of delivery days.

LIKES: Antiques—from Louis XV to Shaker, "super-contemporary" New York penthouses and beach houses, airplanes, opera, Kabuki, skiing, traveling

DISLIKES: Bad reproduction furniture, bedroom suites from Macy's, clutter, pretension, trendy fashion

FAVORITE COLORS: Ivory, black, "natural" colors

LEAST FAVORITE COLORS: The wrong pinks, orange, hospital green

IDEAL CLIENT: Those who say "thank you"

WORST CLIENT: Those who have no confidence in you

RIGHT: Sandra Nunnerley at her light-filled Manhattan office.

LEFT: This elegant and spare bedroom—with its contemporary dropped beams, skylight and fan, and the traditional Shaker bed, flat woven rug, plain walls and sheets—belongs to a contemporary art collector. He wanted his home to highlight artworks that travel back and forth from his New York apartment to his Woodstock, Vermont house. The simplicity of line and purity of color create a harmonious backdrop for his artworks displayed in this gallery/living space. RIGHT: Sandra's bedroom wall is covered with a turn-of-the-century Japanese screen. Decorated with a contemporary lamp, a collection of Japanese vases, a black glass bordered bed, a simple linen bedspread, and rows of pillows—the room brings together several cultures and decorative styles.

ABOVE: A garret was transformed into a lady's boudoir for a Kips Bay show house room. Luxurious and almost ethereal, the sunny room is highlighted by an Italian Directoire bed with silk canopy, pillows, and sheets. The walls were painted with an atmospheric faux finish and adorned with a symmetrically placed crest.

LEFT: The foyer to Sandra's apartment contains a Japanese crackle vase and a Matisse nude. The abstract play of light and dark forms is toned down by the gentle wash of pale pink walls.

SISTER PARISH

One of a kind

If America had "royals," Sister Parish would most certainly be one. Aristocratic in bearing, she personifies Old Money and its attendant values. She numbers among her clients those of blueblood descent and blue-ribbon taste. She does not suffer fools gladly, nor interviews either. Rumor has it that when Jacqueline Kennedy sought the services of Parish-Hadley Associates to decorate The White House, she had to answer more of Sister Parish's questions than she asked.

The only daughter of a well-to-do Morristown, New Jersey family, Dorothy Kinnicut was "sister" to her three brothers; Sister she has remained. Born in 1910, she grew up surrounded by beautiful things. The family traveled to Paris, summered in Maine, and mingled with New York's leading families. Sister looked at the world around her, and she liked what she saw.

Her father was a banker. Following family tradition, she chose a banker for her husband, Henry Parish II. While creating a home for her own family, which grew to include a son and two daughters, Sister launched her career by opening a shop in New Jersey during the Depression. She moved into a tiny New York office in the 1940s, surrounding herself with talented assistants such as Mario Buatta and Mark Hampton. In her partner Albert Hadley, she has named an heir-apparent. Occasionally she threatens to retire. But it's hard to

LEFT: Sister Parish with her dogs, Nanni and Ricky. RIGHT: The Parish apartment is decorated with fine eighteenth-century furnishings, including a rare Axminster rug, a painted glass and gilt English table, Louis XV chairs, a black lacquer table, chairs, and a sofa.

imagine her cut off from her reverent clients and her life's work, content to visit with her eight grandchildren and watch as her dogs, two Pekingese, sniff the air in the courtyard garden of her Fifth Avenue apartment, once the home of screen actress Gloria Swanson.

Sister Parish boasts no academic credentials; she has never been formally schooled in the theory and practice of interior decoration. She says she has simply relied on her instincts. They've clearly served her well, but there's no mistaking the scholarship that underlies her work. Her friendships with such illustrious English decorators as John Fowler, Lady Sybil Colefax, and Nancy Lancaster also proved inspirational

LIKES: Old needlework rugs, old rugs over plain carpets, English-style interiors, a mixture of the old and the new in a room, grand French furniture, French provincial furniture, comfort

DISLIKES: Modern houses, Modern furniture—especially steel furniture, heart-shaped furniture

FAVORITE COLOR: Pale pink

LEAST FAVORITE COLORS: Moody colors

professionally.

If her despotic tendencies and characteristic hauteur are a bit forbidding, her rooms are inviting and charged with grace. The woman best known for her use of luminous colors, flower-strewn fabrics, and rich textures also was responsible for the revival of interest in patchwork quilts and painted wooden stairs.

A Sister Parish house is delightful to visit and delicious to live in. Her predilection for French, Italian, and English eighteenth-century painted furniture and Aubusson, Bessarabian, and Savonnerie rugs coexists with her belief in comfort. She eschews theatrical flourishes. Her houses are warm and welcoming, and surprisingly easy to maintain.

DANIEL PASSEGRIMAUD

Collector's dream

Daniel Passegrimaud of Paris is a collector *extraordinaire*. He has a discerning eye and loves fine paintings, furniture and accessories—especially Russian snuff boxes, gilt and silver objects, and, above all, objects of vertu. He has two kinds of decorating clients: those who collect and those who are just starting to collect. He integrates valued pieces into a room graciously and coherently. "There is nothing worse than having people feel as if they are visiting their own home,"

says Daniel. Straying away from museum-like schemes, his interiors, however, are painstaking recreations of historical modes for living. But these period rooms are meant to be lived in as well as admired. Daniel punctuates them with unusual objects for a lighter touch, and makes every attempt to keep them from becoming stuffy. He chooses objects for their quality or charm. He never allows a "plain" or "standard" element to bring down the tone of a room.

Collectors, Daniel believes, are motivated by curiosity. He is fascinated by furniture that seems completely useless, and collects it with passion. He acquired his untiring love of "things" from his parents, collectors themselves.

Born in Paris on May 31, 1941, Daniel grew up in Vevey, Switzerland. His father was a businessman. After high school, he decided to attend the Louvre School to pursue a career as an art museum curator. In 1964, he was asked to design displays for some Parisian antique dealers. This led to his big break as the decorator of the National Antique Dealer's Association's Biennale exhibition of 1966.

The exhibition was filled with whim-

RIGHT: Daniel Passegrimaud at his office in Paris, next door to the famous Castel nightclub.

sy. Daniel used the style of the late eighteenth and early nineteenth centuries as his base, placing "follies" throughout the exhibition hall (such as a pavilion made entirely of seashells). The French public greeted the effort with enthusiasm, and Daniel emerged as a decorator of imagination and great style. Clients were very intrigued, and his successful business was born.

Daniel's twin obsessions are quality and the idea of discovery. He adores rooms in which the visitor can, in a sense, go on a treasure hunt, finding the special elements one by one. He is also a purist, concerned with the appropriateness of a design scheme or even

LIKES: Russian objects, malachite, hard stones, useless pieces of furniture, textural fabrics, handmade fabrics, movies and theater, bronze, old books, warm and cozy rooms, wood, trompe l'oeil,

DISLIKES: Ostentation, carpets with "long hair," plastics, synthetics, rustic furniture, 1950s and 1960s furniture and decoration, ceramic tiles, sofas that are too low, lacquer, putting a Mexican farm in the middle of the French countryside

LEAST FAVORITE COLORS: Mustard, royal blue

IDEAL CLIENT: Someone who is trusting

WORST CLIENT: There are none. People only get the decorator they deserve!

DREAM PROJECT: To build a neoclassical Palladian house in the south of France

the architecture of a building in relation to where it is geographically. There is nothing worse, in his eyes, than seeing a Mexican farmhouse stuck in the middle of the French countryside, or a Greek temple on the coast of Brittany.

Clients come to appreciate Daniel, not only for his discerning eye, but for his sense of humor, his desire to make rooms that are grand and yet on a human scale, and for his undying devotion to finding exactly the right stuff.

Unimpressed with ostentatious displays of wealth, or worse, collecting for the price tag rather than for personal satisfaction, Daniel is a careful client interviewer. He has learned that a trusting client offers the best relationship during a project. It is his own responsibility, however, to build the kind of trust in a client's eye in order to proceed without mishap. "People only get the decorator they deserve!" he says.

Though always seeking perfection in rooms, Daniel avoids certain elements that he views as perfectly horrible. He feels that rooms that don't have an architectural integrity cannot be furnished properly. Decorating is a subtle art to Daniel, all the elements in a room come together to create a "symphony."

ABOVE: Daniel is a fanatic collector and ardent buyer of eighteenth-century vertu objects and artifacts, as displayed on this table in his sitting room. LEFT: Daniel's office entranceway. The trompe l'oeil painted door attests to his love for unique painted surfaces. RIGHT: Daniel's strong personality takes over in every corner of a room. Quality furniture and objects punctuate his sitting room.

Though this client's Paris sitting room is filled with Charles X furniture and its floor is covered with an Aubusson rug, in Daniel's hands the room doesn't appear too stiff. Instead, its classic elements are brought together in a measured way that is ultimately serene.

NICHOLAS PENTECOST
Traditional ties

N icholas Miles Pentecost work-ed for a decade with the "establishment" decorating firm Parish-Hadley. That experience left a great impression upon him. During his tenure there, he witnessed a way of life that, historically and socially, rarely exists anymore.

When he left the firm to strike out on his own, he maintained a traditional aesthetic, though his style has evolved beyond the English look. Nick is known for rooms that are "interesting"

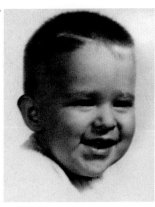

within the format of period decoration. He likes to project a sense of "fancy," adding sparks of interest at key visual points within a composition to enliven a space.

Nick spends much of his time hunting for the right elements of a design scheme. He enjoys searching for antiques and discovering what he calls "treasures." It is this sense of surprise,

and often whimsy, that completes his rooms. "No two jobs are alike," he says. Nick is not "after a look;" he really does try to reproduce people's fantasies.

Nick was born on June 7, 1944 in Los Angeles. His father works in real estate. He attended Whittier College, spending his third year abroad at the University of Copenhagen. A political science and economics major, Nick returned to California for his final undergraduate year. Then he took off for Copenhagen, working in a chemical plant and traveling as much as possible. Returning to California, he landed a job

LIKES: Grand hotels, hunting for antiques, reading, cosiness, gilt furniture, eighteenth- and nineteenth-century Italian and French furniture, Scandinavian furniture, English-style interiors (sans the ribbons and bows), calfskin stenciled to look like leopard skin

DISLIKES: Fussiness, vertical blinds, lucite furniture and lamps, dining tables with glass tops, plastic plants, downlights

FAVORITE COLOR: Red

LEAST FAVORITE COLOR: Blue

IDEAL CLIENT: Friendly, attentive, and professional person

WORST CLIENT: The one with no sense of himself

DREAM PROJECT: To own an antique shop or fabric design company

at a bank in Los Angeles. He was offered the opportunity to move to New York by a bank, and eventually got bored with banking.

Staying in New York, he tried to "find himself." A friend worked for a decorator, and told Nick to try it out. He worked at a small firm for two years, then met Albert Hadley and joined Parish-Hadley. His rise to the top wasn't so easy, however. Nick can recall his worst mistake, ordering a sofa which wouldn't fit into an elevator. It had to be hoisted up along the outside of the building and brought through a window. When in place, the client hated the sofa. Nick had to have it hoisted back down.

LEFT: Nicholas Pentecost. BELOW: Nicholas combines "good things of today with interesting things from the past," such as nineteenth- and twentieth-century oils, a wooden sphinx, and Italian candlestick lamps.

This client's living room overlooks New York's East River. Using washes of black, blue, and green to glaze the silver tea-paper walls, an atmospheric environment is created that elegantly captures the essence of water.

LEFT: The entrance hall is painted in faux stone. Nicholas combined vastly different materials, cultures, and styles in this composition: an eighteenth-century Swedish silver and gilt carved wood console with a marble top, an English Regency *Verre Eglomisee*, a gilt wood mirror, a Californian planter, and a nineteenth-century South African wooden figure.
RIGHT: This eighteenth-century German gilded sunburst and English Regency chair, together with the striped wallpaper, offer a surprisingly contemporary look.

JOSEF PRICCI

English-style comfort

In most decorating circles, it is a mistake to use more than three or four different fabrics in a room. For New York designer Josef Pricci, it is not only a challenge, but a particular joy to find six, or even eight fabrics that work well together. To him, there is a fine line between good and bad taste. Opulent abundance is good taste. Though a confirmed traditionalist and complete anglophile, Josef ventures beyond tassels, fringes, and chintzes. He is flexible enough to use a single fabric selection in a room—if it's appropriate.

Josef is a collector of porcelain and anything associated with man's best friend. Blue-and-white porcelain is a necessary addition to any room, he believes. Dogs, in paintings, on needlepoint pillows, on just about anything, punctuate his well-bred interiors.

For Josef, eighteenth-century English furniture is the backbone of a good room. He appreciates its design purity and is attracted to its sense of history. "Even someone who doesn't know fine furniture can see the quality of a good piece of English furniture," he says.

Josef is a native New

Yorker, born on August 10, 1943. He grew up on Long Island, went to boarding school in Maine, and on to college in Putney, Vermont. An economics major, he felt a bit frustrated, wanting to do something more creative with his life. When he was offered a job as a social events planner at Cartier, he took it. In his four years there, Josef learned a lot about jewelry. He decided to start his own jewelry company. In five years, the firm became very successful, selling to Cartier, Van Cleef & Arpels, and Tiffany & Company. The jewelry Josef designed was very classic in look and a strikingly new approach to the use of semi-precious stones. When he became a decorator, this ability to put things together in new ways became his forte.

Josef likes life in the country, secluded from the headaches of urban life. In his designs, he creates an atmosphere of gentility, in which to pursue beauty.

LIKES: Eighteenth-century English furniture, painted furniture, living well, the ocean, tennis, fringes, tassels, piping

DISLIKES: Bad taste, not knowing when to stop, Modern things, new things

FAVORITE COLORS: Soft pastels, dark green, dark red

IDEAL CLIENT: Has a sense of what is correct

WORST CLIENT: Thinks he has more taste than you do

DREAM PROJECT: To design fabric

LEFT: Josef and his dog Elizabeth in the library of their Park Avenue apartment.

The drawing room of Josef's Manhattan apartment. In the foreground at left is a miniature club chair, a signature element in the decorator's refined English-style room designs.

LEFT: This lavish paneled library, done for a Kips Bay show house, is filled with fine eighteenth-century English antiques. Josef appreciates the purity of line of English furniture. A symphony of fabrics completes the comfortable, stimulating environment. BOTTOM LEFT: This Southampton, New York sun porch is designed for use in any season. Josef liked the composition created using boldly striped curtains against the diamond pattern of the leaded windows. The chintzes make the room bright, even on dreary days. BELOW: Josef adores blue-and-white porcelain. This umbrella stand at his Southampton carriage house is filled with walking sticks, most of which have handles carved in the shape of canine heads.

RIGHT: The bedroom of Josef's New York apartment is hung with an assortment of dog paintings. The tailored monogrammed sheets and pillows and a padded headboard covered in chintz make up a luxurious and comfortable setting from which one can awaken in the city and yet feel cozy and protected.

JOHN SALADINO

Classical scholar

It's not surprising that John Saladino started out to be a painter. His distinguished interiors resonate with the subtle interplay of light and color. John's journey began at the University of Notre Dame in South Bend, Indiana, where he earned a Bachelor of Fine Arts degree. Next, he completed a Master of Fine Arts degree at Yale. What followed, John recalls, was a summer of terror. Without the structure of an academic life, he was filled with uncertainty. For six months, he lived and painted in a Manhattan loft. Though John's color-field canvases attracted a following, success did not mitigate his loneliness. A painter worked alone; John needed to be surrounded by people.

Abandoning the artist's life, John decided to become a decorator. He began with a small firm—shopping for samples, working on blueprints, learning the ropes. At a firm that specialized in commercial projects, John worked on large-scale, complicated designs, developing an understanding of construction.

Born in Kansas City, Missouri, on July 23, 1939, John grew up in a well-to-do family. John's parents were of Italian descent; his father a physician. It was through his older brother Carl that John met Antonio Sartogo, an Italian architect. Sartogo offered John a job in Rome. Immersed in Italian art and architecture, John had the time of his life. Rome taught him a sense of scale and an appreciation of antiquities.

John's commissions are astonishingly diverse. Close to forty percent of his practice is devoted to corporate clients. But his great love is houses: a restoration project in Massachusetts, the decoration of an Arizona ranch, or the design of a New York townhouse. Art collectors, in particular, seek John's services; he often collaborates with architects, designing a house from the inside out so that it will provide an environment sympathetic to a collection.

His talent for synthesizing carefully composed environments from widely disparate elements is legendary. He'll juxtapose period with mod-

LIKES: Slipcovers, overstuffed goosefeather pillows, floor-to-ceiling windows, handblown drinking glasses, faded frescoes, painted panel ceilings, leather floors, oxidized copper urns, old damask fabrics, Italian painted furniture, antiquities

DISLIKES: Chrome coffee tables, oversized lamps, wall-to-wall carpeting, venetian blinds in the home, sliding glass doors, inlaid mother-of-pearl furniture, Victorian furniture, plastic plants, fluorescent lighting in the kitchen

FAVORITE COLORS: Amethyst, celadon, mauve, taupe, beige

LEAST FAVORITE COLOR: Bright yellow

IDEAL CLIENT: A well-educated, visual person with a sense of humor

WORST CLIENT: A neurotic person who is unable to relax

DREAM PROJECT: To mount an exhibition of his paintings

RIGHT: Decorator John Saladino at his elegant Manhattan apartment on Park Avenue.

ern furniture, Greek and Roman artifacts with sleek surfaces, the rare and luxurious with the humble and minimal. Everything will work together, the mover's quilt hung like a tapestry, the oversized sofas, the trompe l'oeil doors.

A gregarious man, John keeps his business and social life separate. The decorator-client relationship, however, is intense. Sometimes, he says, you inadvertently become involved in your client's life. Once his office was barraged with calls from a woman he had never met who wanted information about a client whose big, important house he was then decorating. To keep the peace, he finally took her call. "I've just returned from your client's house," she said breathlessly. "He asked me to marry him. I know you're his decorator so maybe you can answer some questions I have about him." John was intrigued; so far as he knew, his client was vacationing in Palm Beach, awaiting the completion of his house. John called Palm Beach and spoke to his client who, roaring with laughter, explained, "My driver's

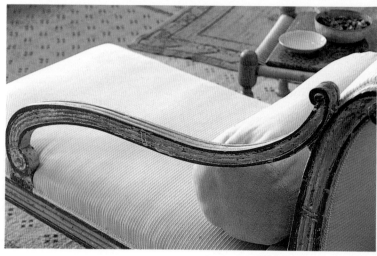

up to his old tricks again." While John's client was away, the driver spent his time picking up women by posing as the owner of the impressive house.

John first came to New York City when he was twenty-three. He married his wife Virginia, also an interior decorator, in 1969, opened his own office in the city, and lived with his wife and son in a palatial Park Avenue apartment, repairing on weekends to their Connecticut house with its beautiful garden. He dreams of creating a garden that will live on after him, a living legacy for his son. Following the death of his wife in 1988, John is moving in that direction. He now spends a great deal of time at his new home in Santa Barbara, growing his beautiful garden there, longing to spend more time at his painting easel.

LEFT: The painted wood grillwork in the Saladino dressing room was designed by John. The repeating starburst shapes play off against the curvilinear Xs of the French Napoleon I campaign chairs. ABOVE: One of two Italian récamier in John's Manhattan bedroom. The slow curves of the chair arms, the geometric patterning of the Oriental rugs, and the rounded curves of the table's frame create a subtle rhythm. RIGHT: The lamps on this Italian painted console were designed by John. Together with an architectural model and framed mirror, they form a striking tabletop landscape. The wall behind is texturally stuccoed and painted.

LEFT: Simple, yet refined textures—crumpled paper-like surfaces and quilted folds—create a new look for upholstery and wallcoverings that almost parody tradition. This Saladino-designed living room has a sedate and thoughtful quality to it that surprisingly harmonizes with the more traditional room beyond. RIGHT: The living room blends textures and patterns. Sofa cushions and upholstery and wall surfaces are tastefully coordinated to create the effect of spaciousness. The lamp and sofa are Saladino custom designs.

LEFT: This carved fireplace and mantel, on which are displayed an architectural maquette and small sculpted figures, represents John's more traditionally oriented side. Because his own furniture designs are minimal in line, he is able to successfully combine them with period pieces for a fresh look. ABOVE: A dining room reserved for the Puritan in spirit, until one notices the discreet proportions of the gracefully elongated dining table and chair, and the slightly curved corners of the side table. A classical, yet thoroughly contemporary approach makes John's work especially appealing.

BELOW: The Tripod table, seen from above, exhibits John's ability to combine fundamental shapes for an exquisitely refined result. RIGHT: The Balustrade table, also a John Saladino design, has a classic appeal. Both pieces are sold to the trade through the Saladino Furniture showroom in New York City.

RIGHT: The Amphora lamp is a signature piece from John's own collection of furnishings available through his showroom/office in New York City.

ABOVE: The Porticus bench, designed by John Saladino. It has a strong presence, and yet is delicately detailed. John's custom furniture designs, once offered only to clients, are now available through his showroom, for those who can appreciate the Saladino look.

BELOW: The Tulip chair, a John Saladino furniture design, has a minimal, understated form. Its proportions and tailored detailing give it a fascinating sense of lightness and gravity—a chair you can sink into without being smothered. Many decorators design custom furniture for clients. John has taken that concept a step further, by creating the Saladino Furniture Collection, available to other members of the trade.

DAVID SALOMON

Exotic flavor

A bare room is like a blank canvas for decorating "artist" David Salomon of New York City. He combines furniture, objects, and finishes to achieve a layered, yet harmonious "composition" for his clients.

David might be called an orientalist. He expertly inserts exotic elements in his room designs, intrigued by the rich patterning of fabrics, carpets, and objects from the Far East, India, and North Africa.

Born in Oak Park, Illinois on July 26, 1949, David studied painting, first at Drake University in Des Moines, Iowa, and then at the School of the Art Institute in Chicago. He moved to New York, eventually taking a job in the interior design department of Bonwit Teller. The wife of the president of the store asked for David's assistance in decorating her own apartment. Thoroughly pleased with David's abilities, she went on to recommend him to her friends who were in need of decorating help. After a while, David had an established base of clients and a business.

Perhaps this designer can trace his decorating roots to his grandfather, who was an

expert cabinetmaker, and with whom David spent many hours as a child. David's great knowledge of furniture styles was further honed through his association with the great English decorator Geoffrey Bennison, whom he met through Françoise de la Renta, a fabulous hostess and tastemaker in Manhattan. Mrs. de la Renta introduced David to Marie-Hélène de Rothschild, for whom Bennison was designing a New York apartment. Bennison needed a responsible assistant on the job. David was hired on the spot. Bennison encouraged David to "unleash his talent." For David, the example Bennison set has forever been engraved in his mind. "Geoffrey Bennison was capable of decorating a palace and making it seem like a home," he remarks. David embraced that philosophy, creating rooms both calm and quirky—like the people he feels most comfortable working with. His talent stems from his excellent instincts and his ability to see a room, like a painter sees a painting, in his mind before he steps in with the proper furnishings.

LIKES: Warm, cozy rooms, the sea, fabric, elaborate patterns, one "good" object, rugs, paintings, flowers, seashells

DISLIKES: White-background chintz, balloon shades, kitchens and bathrooms, glazed walls, things that look brand new, chrome

FAVORITE COLOR: Red

LEAST FAVORITE COLORS: Yellow, purple

IDEAL CLIENT: Someone who trusts you implicitly

WORST CLIENT: One with bad taste

DREAM PROJECT: To design for the theater

LEFT: New York decorator David Salomon, seated in a chair designed by his grandfather, in front of the fireplace of his Upper West Side apartment.

The rich play of kilim rug patterns on the sofa and curtains of this large paneled sitting room contribute to its overall atmosphere of luxury. Touches of gilt and a variety of "good" nineteenth-century portraits of women add to the desired effect of opulence combined with the exotic.

On the fireplace mantel of David's tiny brownstone apartment in New York—his laboratory for design ideas—a number of unrelated items are expertly grouped together, including a papier-maché carnival mask by Robert Courtwright, a nineteenth-century bronze figure of an athlete, and small framed drawings by David. Reflected in the mirror behind are a wall hanging from Mali, a painting of a table done by David at age 16, and the stenciled walls of his apartment, created in collaboration with artist Gail Leddy.

HENRI SAMUEL

Enduring quality

For serious collectors of art and antiquities, owners of imposing, historic houses, and those with a passion for architecture and decoration informed by scholarship and taste, Henri Samuel is the designer nonpareil. He has worked for many decades with prestigious clients, creating decorative arts galleries for the Metropolitan Museum of Art and Versailles and splendid homes for the Rothschilds, Vanderbilts, and Hearsts. His museum rooms are consummate period pieces, masterful evocations of the past. His homes are a heady mix of furnishings and art, a celebration of diversity.

Henri was born in Paris in January 1904. He and his brother and sister grew up in a family that included art dealers and collectors. But Henri was groomed to follow in the footsteps of his father, a banker. After completing his education in Paris, his father sent him off to New York to work as a stockbroker. Two years later Henri returned to France and told his family that the world of finance was not for him; instead, inspired by his strong visual sense and his appreciation for the art collections with which he had been surrounded as a child, Henri determined to become a decorator.

After completing military service, Henri went to work with the legendary Mr. Boudin of Jansen, a firm that was at the peak of its impressive reputation in the mid-1920s. Jansen's client list was international, with commissions in Buenos Aires, Cairo, Havana, London, and New York. Henri went on to work at two important Parisian decorating companies, Ramsey and Alavoine, before opening his own firm in 1970.

The hallmark of an Henri Samuel design project is quality. His interiors for hotels, yachts, museums, and private houses share an appreciation for excellence, for the well-made, the well-finished. He urges his clients to buy only the best; the period of a piece of furniture is not as important as the quality it embodies. Entering a room Henri decorated twenty years earlier, you're struck by how wonderful everything looks. His rooms age gracefully.

Henri's distinguished career and client list attest to his mastery of the design business. You need to be a diplomat, he says, to work with many different clients.

LIKES: The Modern period, mixing styles, opera, Louis XIV and Louis XVI furniture, Gothic-revival style, Directoire period, natural fabrics

DISLIKES: Louis XV furniture, a room that looks "decorated"

FAVORITE COLOR: Mauve

LEAST FAVORITE COLOR: Bordeaux

LEFT: Henri Samuel, with his dachshunds, in Paris.

The sitting room features a Balthus painting, Giacometti table, and numerous fine objects that Henri has collected over many years. INSET: Details are at the heart of a Samuel design. Here, at the floor level of his own Paris library, a fine tole wood basket is nestled next to the feet of a carved Egyptian figure.

ABOVE: Henri's eclectically decorated library contains a French Empire armchair and a sculpture of a peasant woman. Both pieces illustrate Henri's fascination with delicate surface details within the context of an entire roomscape. RIGHT: An intricately carved, Empire fireplace in the Egyptian taste is a focal point of Henri's sitting room in Paris. Furnishings, such as the contemporary cocktail table and a fine Louis XVI armchair offer testament to Henri's subtle, refined eye and his great ability to combine periods within a single room.

BETTY SHERRILL

A sure hand

Betty Sherrill, president of McMillen, the venerable New York decorating firm, combines the best attributes of a no-nonsense executive and a privileged Southern lady. Her clients, from Old Money families to Middle Eastern royalty, often become her friends. Her friends then call on her as they move from one house to another, one generation to the next.

Born in New Orleans on April 18, 1924, Betty grew up in a well-established family. She attended private school and Sophie Newcomb College, where she learned as much as she could about art and history. Her father and grandfather were both architects.

Shortly after her marriage in 1949 to Virgill Sherill, she found herself living in New York, homesick and bored. To fill the hours, she enrolled at the Parsons School of Design.

Diploma in hand, she struck out on her own, opening Elizabeth Sherrill Interiors. Her next stop was the East 50th Street brownstone that housed McMillen, a solid, socially connected decorating establishment. For 15 years she served as assistant to Mrs. Smith, who's now been a member of the firm for sixty years. Following in the footsteps of her inspiration, Mrs. Brown, the founder of McMillen, Betty became part owner and president.

While Betty's firm has a decidedly old-school flavor and her own work is classic in nature, there's nothing stuffy about her houses. Betty genuinely likes people. Her Southern heritage, with its accent on quality of life and gracious hospitality, makes her especially adept at designing settings for entertaining and conversation.

There is no Betty Sherrill "look." She's careful not to force anything on her clients. For clients who are young or not particularly aware of period furniture, art, or design, Betty adores her role as trainer. She'll teach them the value of quality, with an eye on practicality as well. Betty Sherrill keeps the McMillen traditions alive and her clients happy.

LIKES: Red flowers, good quality or charming needlepoint rugs and pillows, beautiful reproduction furniture, Chinese coffee tables, Venetian crystal mirrors, round dining tables, draped tables, wall-to-wall carpeting in bedrooms, polished floors in reception rooms, undisguised television sets and telephones (They are facts of life, why hide them?)

DISLIKES: Rugs on top of rugs, fifteen pillows on a sofa, artificial flowers, host and hostess chairs at a dining table, period rooms, Aubusson carpets, shawls, gold plumbing fixtures

FAVORITE COLORS: White, yellow (but not in bedrooms)

LEAST FAVORITE COLORS: Autumnal colors

IDEAL CLIENT: One with varied interests who is imaginative, knowledgeable, and stylish

WORST CLIENT: A rigid person

DREAM PROJECT: To design low-income housing

LEFT: Betty Sherrill in her comfortable New York living room. A portrait of her mother-in-law hangs in the background.

LEFT: Betty's living room contains many period pieces. The carved fireplace and frame are Louis XVI. The embroidered ballroom chair, bronze candelabra, and candlestick clock are nineteenth-century French pieces. The Chinese porcelain vase and Raymond Le Geult painting are twentieth-century touches. The subtle combination of various traditions suggests Betty's sensitivity to good design whatever its epoch. RIGHT: Central to this spacious and sunny Texas living room is the large blue and coral patterned antique Sultana rug. The furniture and decorative objects were selected to complement its luxurious pattern without competing with it. Coral touches—a modern silk damask sofa, velvet antique English chairs, and taffeta drapes—unify the large space. Reflective antique crystal sconces and lamps create an essential "quality" of light. Chinese porcelain, a Raymond Le Geult painting, and an English veneered table balance the room. BOTTOM RIGHT: This airy, green, black, and white porch has a multipurpose function. The clients dine there privately and can also formally entertain up to thirty guests. They are known to roll up the zebra skin rugs for dancing. The dividing wall, originally glass, now contains a niche to store and display the couple's porcelain collection. The porch's decor draws from French, English, Chinese, and contemporary sources.

STEPHEN SILLS

Zestfully muted

T here's more than a little spirit of the Wild West in Stephen Sills's work. The Oklahoma-born decorator brings to his neoclassical interiors an outlaw's glamorous bravado, a fearlessness, a sense of freedom. A master of legerdemain, he brings wit and fantasy to his rooms.

A civilized country boy, Stephen was born on May 20, 1953 and grew up in Durant, Oklahoma. His mother was a concert pianist who taught music on the university level; his father was an optha-

mologist. After high school in Durant, he set off for North Texas University, where he learned next to nothing, he recalls, except discipline. He moved to Paris, where he came alive. Stephen had dreamed of becoming a painter, but he found his calling after apprenticing with Renzo Mongiardino. Renzo was the perfect teacher—a mentor whose grasp of atmosphere and architecture remain a source of Stephen's inspiration.

After Paris, Stephen moved to Dallas and worked briefly with an established decorator before launching his own firm. In 1985, tired of Texas, Stephen opened his New York office. His primary commissions have been residences in the fashionable Hamptons, Connecticut, and New York City.

LEFT: Stephen Sills in Central Park. RIGHT: Stephen's former apartment, with its decorative turn-of-the-century fireplace, Egyptian antiquities, and Man Ray photographs, has a very unusual appeal. The particular styles of individual pieces remain distinct from each other—neither harmonizing nor creating a sense of discord. Stephen's style is strong and personal.

LIKES: Traveling to exotic places, Italian painted furniture, Russian brass-and-mahogany furniture, Arts & Crafts furniture, Gothic furniture, old gilded mirrors, Fortuny fabrics, French handwoven linen

DISLIKES: Bright paint colors, new mirrors, color-coordinated design schemes, brown English and American furniture, overstuffed chairs and sofas, glitzy interiors, bad art (would rather have no art at all), too many candlesticks, garish printed fabrics, the Hollywood version of English-country style

FAVORITE COLORS: Bisque white, deep Pompeian colors

LEAST FAVORITE COLORS: Easter-egg pastels

IDEAL CLIENT: Creative, with great taste

WORST CLIENT: Unappreciative ones

DREAM PROJECT: To design a hotel in Fiji

LEFT: For a Kips Bay show house room, Stephen combined traditional and folk arts, and precious and everyday objects for a powerful display of cultural artifacts. This collection includes: a bronze spear from Tangier, an eighteenth-century Italian painting, a turn-of-the-century drawing, plaques found at a Paris flea market, a Russian egg, and African money. RIGHT: This antique-filled Kips Bay show house room was designed as a collector's bedroom. The overall effect is traditional, with discreet modern touches such as the geometrical composition formed by the vertical line of framed nineteenth-century drawings and the wall trimming.

ABOVE: Stephen's Texas library is furnished with a generously cushioned sofa, period furniture, and a modern lamp. The detailing on the relatively empty walls is emphasized, providing a quiet, uncluttered, introspective space. LEFT: This Manhattan apartment radically juxtaposes shapes, styles, and traditions. The boldly striped walls create a striking backdrop for a seventeenth-century framed needlework picture. A portrait bust and plant rest on a table bordered with triangles.

SISKIN/VALLS

Spicy haute couture

Sparseness without frugality; luxury without costliness; fashion without trendiness—these concepts underly the work of Paul Siskin and Perucho Valls. "Conceptual artists" who don't rely too heavily on the concepts, the two men are excellent aesthetic companions. Perucho adores glamour and fantasy, while Paul has an understanding of what works and what doesn't. The result is a sophisticated blend of flash and restraint. Their slipcovers, for instance, are brilliant twists on what was once a rather dowdy and economical approach to covering furniture. The slipcovers look like dresses, or in Magritte-like instances, are printed with chair patterns—transforming a reproduction chair into a masterpiece.

Perucho, born in Caracas, Venezuela, is the "spoiled," only son of a building contractor and his politically active wife. He studied dance, at one time traveling to Russia on tour with the Caracas Ballet. Perucho came to New York in the 1970s, landing a job as Halston's assistant. Under

Halston's tutelage, Perucho learned about the use of color and proportion in design. Perucho's fashion background has served him well. His expert knowledge of fabric draping, for instance, is creatively applied to "room-dressing."

Paul is a Los Angeles native. His grandfather founded the largest furniture manufacturing firm in the Los Angeles basin. Paul's father continued with the family business and when he became old enough, Paul joined his father's firm as an antiques buyer. He went to Colorado State University, obtaining a Bachelor's degree in Sociology. He moved to New York City in 1974, enrolling

at the Parsons School of Design. While still a student, Paul worked in the office of John Saladino.

In 1986, Paul and Perucho joined forces, opening their own office. Their design doctrine is "Never say never," which keeps their designs fresh, and their clients surprised.

RIGHT: Perucho Valls (left) and Paul Siskin costumed as Regency chairs. The trompe l'oeil leopard and faux damask blue paisley slipcovers are of their own design.

LIKES: Cashmere in the winter, cotton in the summer, flowers, to mix and twist things, black dresses, Tiffany candles

DISLIKES: Plastic, silk, and porcelain flower arrangements, anything laminated, pretension, period rooms, clutter

FAVORITE COLORS: Ivory, cream, gold

LEAST FAVORITE COLORS: Bright red, chartreuse, shocking pink

IDEAL CLIENT: One with a sense of humor

WORST CLIENT: The one who is a bully

DREAM PROJECT: To design sets for the theater or the ballet

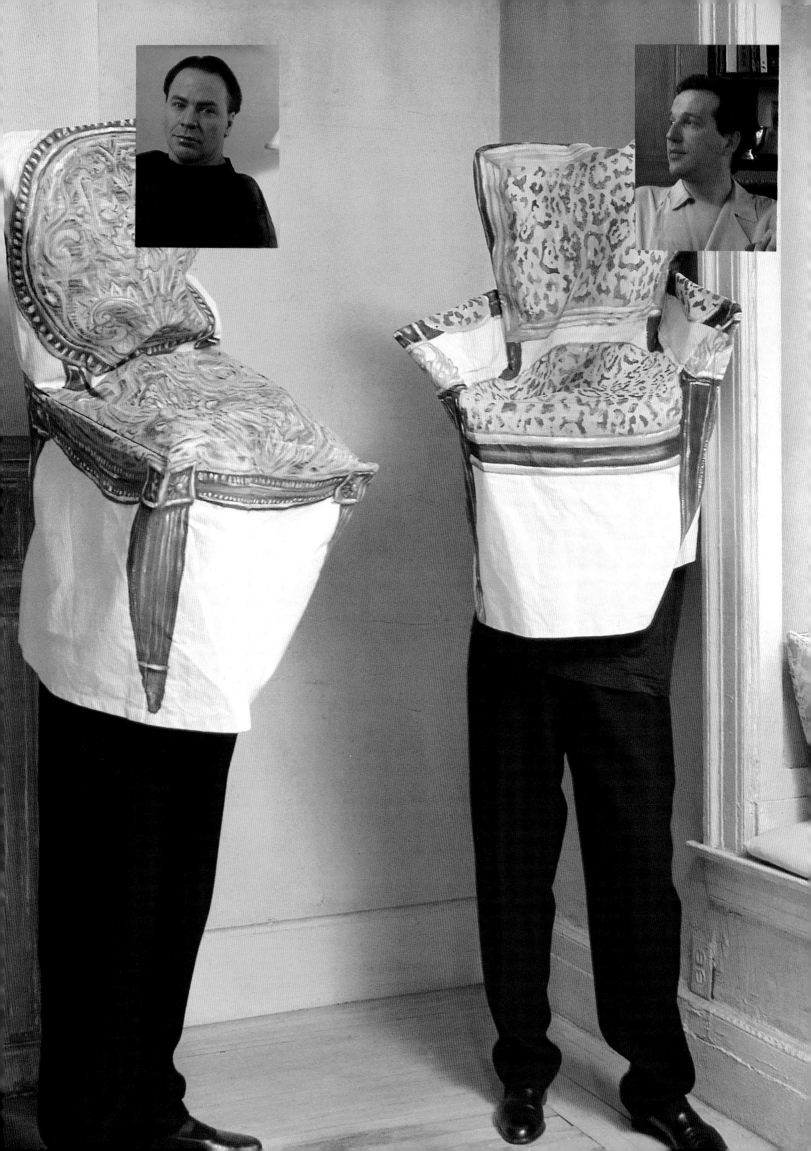

LEFT: A glimpse at Perucho's bedroom testifies to his background in fashion, and his love of the dramatic and fantastic. Here he keeps his collection of illustrations and photographs, ivory brushes, masks, hats—and a shoe sculpture. BOTTOM LEFT: Paul is more conceptually and functionally oriented. His apartment was once a townhouse library. The pine walls were stripped and left raw. A personal computer and a mud shoe sculpture both rest on a nineteenth-century provincial Italian kitchen table. The brass desk lamp with cantilevers is an Italian prototype from the fifties—a "failed" design that Paul admires for its pure form. RIGHT: Both Paul and Perucho love Tiffany Studio candlesticks, which they see as the epitome of elegance and simplicity. The fired English ceramic plate contains assorted metal balls for a subtle play of surfaces.

LEFT: This quiet but studied composition exemplifies Siskin and Valls's tendency to mix and combine elements from other times and places rather than to reproduce the look of a particular era. This gold-on-brass Tiffany Studio candlestick has a stippled finish. Curving alongside it is a nineteenth-century Japanese turquoise-eyed fish. RIGHT: The walls of Paul and Perucho's office were purposely treated to convey a state of disrepair. The surface was sealed and covered with light gradations of an umber, ochre, and sienna wash, creating a "rainwashed effect." The pine fireplace was chipped to undo its air of newness. On the mantelpiece stand a seventeenth-century wooden column, a nineteenth-century French dressmaker's doll, a Tiffany Studio candlestick and a twenties brass sconce.

ETHEL SMITH

Toast of the old guard

A true New Yorker—Ethel Smith, of the venerable Manhattan decorating firm McMillen, was born in 1905 on the East Side of Manhattan. After a "good" education at an Englewood, New Jersey boarding school, Ethel was "pushed" by an aunt toward a career in interior decoration. The effort proved unnecessary, however. Ethel had always loved the decorative arts.

Ethel enrolled in the New York School of Fine and Applied Arts (now the Parsons School), spending her third year of studies in Paris—with her aunt along as a proper chaperone. Her schooling included trips to all the grand houses of England and France. Ethel also traveled to Italy, discovering its beauty. At the time, she wondered how she could possibly use all that she'd seen and learned. Now, she knows that the experience taught her about proper proportion in design, something that has to be seen rather than explained.

Ethel worked for Macy's briefly, and then with decorator Margaret Owen. It was under Mrs. Owen's employ that Ethel gained her extraordinary ability to picture in her mind a room's decor right from the beginning of a project—down to the last ashtray. She explains: "She had a tiny office. One could not set out four or five samples at a time there—you had to organize it all in your head."

Her career with McMillen

DISLIKES: Fancy lampshades, pillows on the floor in a room corner

FAVORITE COLOR: Yellow

LEAST FAVORITE COLOR: Old rose

IDEAL CLIENT: The one who knows his own mind

WORST CLIENT: The one who cannot make up his mind

began in 1929. Under Eleanor Brown's tutelage, she developed into a versatile designer. The McMillen look is not static. Over the years the firm has addressed the decoration of a house in many ways, though always with a taste for quality. Trends may come and go, such as "witty plastic furniture," but Mc-Millen decorators are astute editors who "weed out" the trendy, seeking out styles of furnishings that will last.

An Ethel Smith room is comfortable, well detailed, and "truly" decorated. Quality and practicality are inherent elements in her designs. She loves diversity, having decorated yachts, shops, ballrooms, and country cottages. Ethel is also an improviser. It is part of her

skill, borne from experience.

She remembers her first mistake. For a house in St. Louis, she had curtains made for the dining room, using a very expensive silk fabric. When the time came to hang them, she discovered that the curtains were too short. She immediately added a foot of fringe to the bottom—a quick solution. Twenty years later, the clients called, needing new curtains. They asked, "Could we have precisely the same thing, with twelve inches of fringe on the bottom?" Mistakes become cherished details in this decorator's hands.

LEFT: Ethel Smith. ABOVE RIGHT: A collection of precious items on Ethel's bedroom bureau. BELOW: For Ethel this large and sunny living room is perfect for lounging quietly with her family or entertaining a large group. Plaster shells along the ceiling provide an indirect source of light and, together with bronze seagulls, create a continuity with the outdoors.

JEROME SUTTER

In the French tradition

With his ties to the world of opera, it is no wonder that rooms decorated by Jerome Sutter are theatrical and grand. Steeped in the traditions of the regal French life-style, with classical Louis-style rooms as his forte, they are formal, palatial, and always "correct."

Jerome was born in Malleray, Switzerland on March 4, 1928. His father was an importer of French food. At eighteen, Jerome left Switzerland for Paris. The year was 1946, and Paris was in a state of rebirth after the scars of the Second World War and the Occupation. He enrolled in the Beaux-Arts academy, but stopped after three years to pursue a career in photography, eventually working as a freelancer for newspapers and magazines.

It was through filmmaker Francois Reichenbach that Jerome discovered his chosen profession. Jerome met Reichenbach during the war while the director was hiding out in Switzerland to escape from the Nazis. Jerome traveled to locations, working as part of the crew for the film, *L'Amérique Insolite*, about life in the United States.

In 1958, Jerome began a long association with the Dallas Opera as an artistic consultant. He was responsible for the sets, fur-

nishings, and costumes. As an integral part of an emerging opera company, Jerome worked with some of the finest names on the international scene—Franco Zeffirelli, Maria Callas, Placido Domingo, and Joan Sutherland.

In 1977, Jerome opened his own showroom in New York, selling lacquer furniture and accessories. He maintained the business for five years, developing a client list at the same time. In 1982, he closed the showroom, devoting himself exclusively to private clients. He commutes regularly between New York and Paris.

When not at work decorating his "palaces," Jerome can be found tinkering in the garden. One can imagine, however, that his garden, like his rooms, is painstakingly designed.

LIKES: Gardening, lacquer furniture
DISLIKES: Mediocrity
FAVORITE COLORS: Coral red, blue, yellow
IDEAL CLIENT: A person who wants to participate in the conception and design of a project

RIGHT: Jerome Sutter on the staircase of his Paris apartment, located in a "haute bourgeois" 1870s building. In his baby picture, above, he is seated at center between his older sister and brother.

LEFT: Jerome's study is filled with fine artworks and objects. The Venetian painting is framed in tortoiseshell. On the mahogany console, a pair of bronze horses and Bouilotte lamps are displayed. A bronze atlas supports an armillary sphere. Objects are arranged in quiet symmetry, shown off to their best advantage in the soft light reflected from the upholstered walls.

ABOVE: A collector for over two decades, Jerome's Paris home is a place of discovery. A Louis XVI cylindrical desk in the library displays many of his finds, including a bronze figure of Marcus Aurelius on horseback, bisque sphinxes—representations of Madame du Barry and Madame du Pompadour, a gilt bronze coach clock, a Chantilly porcelain inkstand, and a rare Meissen rhinoceros.
LEFT: This corner of Jerome's Paris sitting room is furnished with a Louis XVI leather upholstered armchair and draped table, on which a collection of bronze figures is displayed. Fresh flowers add a touch of nature. A lovely Renoir pastel is set off by the mottled walls.

DADDO TORRIGIANI

A taste for architecture

In Italy, the term "decorator" is not often used. An *architetto* trained at a university is well versed in all aspects of design: industrial, architectural, interior, graphic, and furniture. Once out of the university, most graduates specialize in one of the fields, but it is not uncommon for a designer to be involved in, by North American standards, a multidisciplinary practice. The Milan-based designer Daddo Torrigiani is such a professional. His clients come to him to design a house inside and out.

His process of design differs from convention, however. Daddo sees the interior of the house as his first priority. It is where the client will actually live. When the interior is complete, he moves on to embellish the exterior of the house, villa, boat, or hotel. Daddo's interiors feature bold, clear, and strong colors. In furnishing a room, he mixes the classics with the contemporary, gearing the atmosphere of a home or apartment to its owner's personality and particular, or even peculiar tastes.

Born in Modena, Italy on August 27, 1928, Daddo is the son of a cavalry officer who became a prominent antique dealer in Milan. Daddo's father was one of the first Italian dealers to import English furniture in the mid-1930s. As an only child, Daddo studied architecture in Milan, receiving his diploma in 1953. He immediately opened a studio with two friends from the university. Today, he and one of his three sons, also trained as an architect, run the Torrigiani design business. In addition to the architectural work the office is involved in, Daddo finds the time to write poetry, design beautiful

RIGHT: Architect Daddo Torrigiani on the terrace of his beautiful Milan apartment.

glass objects for manufacturers, and design magnificent lacquered furniture. He enjoys his independence, and the ability to choose his projects carefully. He would never want to work for just anyone.

Daddo has eclectic taste. He loves antiques from Italy, France, and England. He is an expert at picking the right stone or marble for an installation. Within an architectural framework that is simple and extremely functional, Daddo places pieces chosen carefully for comfort as well as for style. There isn't an ounce of pretension present in a Torrigiani room. He is repulsed by people who try to show off their money through their homes, and he doesn't tolerate so-

cial climbers. Daddo is a great collector. His architect's eye, and childhood exposure to the finer aspects of the decorative arts allow him to creatively assist clients in putting coherent rooms together that are not only beautiful, but also individual. Daddo also has great respect for artists (painting is another one of his many pastimes) and is extremely careful about the way in which art is integrated into the living space. "Paintings should always be hung prominently and straight," he says. And, of course, any art included as part of a decorating scheme should have meaning to its owner.

Daddo's first decorating disaster occurred during the Christmas season. He had designed a winter garden room for a client friend. On December 24, Daddo arrived at the client's home, preparing the house for the next evening's festivities. Taking a break, he casually lit a cigarette. Somehow, a fire started. He called for help, managed to put out the fire, and promptly set out to redo the room in twenty-four hours. He ran all over the city of Milan on Christmas Day to replace what had been damaged by the fire. Luckily, he was able to replace the contents of the room—down to the last ashtray. The client arrived Christmas night and never knew that disaster had struck.

LEFT: Daddo is drawn to strong colors. His blue and red master bedroom is a case in point. RIGHT: Thoroughly contemporary, Daddo's kitchen is another bright spot in the designer's apartment. Daddo sees kitchens as places where an entirely modern vocabulary can take over. FAR RIGHT: The whimsical objects on display in the kitchen include old eyeglasses, purses, and jewelry. BOTTOM RIGHT: Blue sets the tone for Daddo's comfortably cluttered dining room.

HERBERT WELLS

Texas-style sophistication

Working for "just about everyone who counts" among Houston's business and social elite, decorator Herbert Wells has proven to be the city's most influential designer. When his competitors were producing strictly period rooms, he took a more contemporary approach, custom fabricating steel furniture and introducing a less stuffy, more appropriate style to the Texas public. Many of the properties he is called upon to decorate are "new," lacking the history, charm, and details of older homes. His solutions don't impose a false history on a home. He retains the contemporary "envelope," mixing old and new elements within it. The idea of a purely traditional environment just doesn't seem correct to him.

For Herbert, "most of the rules of decoration have to be ignored; you have to have enough confidence in yourself to ignore them." He uses color as a key element in his designs. He says, "a good color doesn't cost any more to use than a poor one—you had better use the good one!"

Herbert was born in the Boston suburb of Winthrop, Massachusetts on January 25, 1924. He and his older brother were raised in Hartford, Connecticut. His father was involved in the insurance business. He left high school, and worked in a department store as a window dresser. In 1950, he moved to Houston, seeing better opportunities for work there. Working in a department store, he initially hated what he called "the provincialism" of the Texas city. He overcame his dislike for the place, however, and decided to open his own business, designing ladies hats. "It was the least expensive business to start," he recalls, "and that's why I chose it." It was a very successful business, and little by little, Herbert switched gears, beginning first with the selling of decorative fabrics, then furniture and objects. Finally, Herbert was a force on the Houston decorating scene. His brother was capable of running the shop, so Herbert turned his efforts over to decorating for clients in 1952. He has an intuitive sense about what works and what does not, and this brought him to favor with the cultured elite of the city.

LIKES: Good lighting, good Modern paintings, a mixture of old and new, painted furniture

DISLIKES: Bad art, purely traditional rooms, waste (as when the lining of a curtain is more expensive than the curtain fabric itself), deadlines, "special" effects

FAVORITE COLORS: Khaki, pale blue, shades of white

LEAST FAVORITE COLORS: Wine, red, maroon

IDEAL CLIENT: Someone you know very well who is open to suggestions

WORST CLIENT: Unresponsive, set in their ways

DREAM PROJECT: To restore a townhouse

LEFT: Herbert Wells in the lush garden of his Houston home.

LEFT: A beautiful folding screen can add dimension to a room rather than simply concealing space. This Japanese screen provides Herbert's formal dining room with a stylized, cheerful still-life. Its stark, solid background partially "stills" the wallpaper's busier intersecting lines. RIGHT: A garden room with outrageous style. The bold, playful lines and curves of this papier-maché column, designed for a theater, and a painted canvas by Jack Boynpon, have only the graceful presence of these eighteenth-century French stools to restrain them.

ABOVE: Finials, to Herbert, are artworks in their own right. His collection contains finials made of various materials, including these made of wood and steel.

LEFT: This delicate box, fabricated from bone, resembles a pagoda. Behind it, a Modern painting is on display. BELOW: Herbert commissioned these tiles, molded of blue concrete. Their grainy texture enhances the surfaces of the steel urn and French chair.

BUNNY WILLIAMS

A *warm, shining star*

"You have to know how to break the rules, but in order to do that, you first must know the rules very well," states Manhattan decorator Bunny Williams. Bunny creates interiors where you can put your feet up. Though knowledgeable about furniture, her warm and inviting rooms are not "caught up" in ostentatious displays of wealth. She is a brilliant shopper, and isn't snobbish about her sources. If something at a flea market catches her eye, she will readily buy it, insert it into a room scheme, even highlight it, because, to her, it is the effect, not the price tag that she and her clients are concerned with.

It goes without saying that Bunny likes quality, but her talent lies in her ability to inject charm into a space, and a lot of personality. She is also an expert colorist, able to bring colors together that would seemingly clash, unafraid of so-called strange colors that one doesn't see too much, like purples and greens—"hard combinations" in many other decorators' eyes. She mixes strong dark colors with traditional chintzes. She fills a room with an eclectic array of furnishings—an English regency table, Swedish chairs, a French dining table, Russian chairs. Bunny views her personal style as traditionally based, but not a pure English style, more of an American-adapted taste.

Bunny is originally from Charlottesville, Virginia, born on November 1, 1943. She and her brother grew up in a household where design was always a priority. This sophisticated interest in design stemmed from the fact that her businessman father was a "frustrated" architect, she supposes.

Bunny didn't go to design school, she had some of the best on-the-job training possible. When she moved to New York to attend college (where she lasted only one year), she was eager to get "real life" started. Her initial entrance into the decorating business was at an antique dealer. She then heard that decorator Albert Hadley needed a secretary. Though she didn't know how to type, Hadley hired her. Starting at the bottom of Parish-Hadley's hierarchy, she learned a lot about decorating through her twenty-two years there. She eventually became one of the Parish-Hadley team. Recently, she struck out on her own.

LIKES: Traditional but not just English style, antiques, painted furniture, odd combinations

DISLIKES: Collections that are just for show, choosing a home for its address, decorators who are dictators

FAVORITE COLORS: Purple and green, late-Regency colors: dusty green and turquoise

IDEAL CLIENT: Those who become friends

DREAM PROJECT: To build a house from the ground up

RIGHT: Bunny Williams at her Manhattan home.

LEFT: Bunny's living room contains two Italian period pieces. The seventeenth-century painting still has its original carved and painted wooden frame. Upon the eighteenth-century console table Bunny has symmetrically arranged a composition using flowers, marble obelisks, tole *gardeniers*, photographs, and magazines. The choice of objects displayed on this console demonstrates a love of both nature and order, and at the same time includes items that are personal and everyday. This is very much in keeping with Bunny's belief that life should not be controlled by design. BOTTOM LEFT: Although this large bedroom with chintz covered walls contains several English pieces, it is less a period room than a space offering comfort and peace of mind. A magnificent early-nineteenth-century English four-poster bed with painted canopy, an English mahogany chest, and a painted mirror purchased at a thrift store are reflected in the large oval mirror of Bunny's nineteenth-century satinwood dressing table. Family photos and Bunny's collection of antique porcelain rabbits are arranged below. RIGHT: Indian prints, in antique walnut frames, hang on the rich green lacquered walls of Bunny's dining room/library. A porcelain bowl, carved wooden cow, and numerous photographs are arranged on top of the painted American table. For Bunny, beauty follows function—as demonstrated by the Chinese vase that she had converted into a lamp.

LEFT: Family photographs are hung on either side of a carved and gilded wood Regency sunburst clock in the Williams apartment. RIGHT: In the living/dining room, a Biedermeier mirror reflects the bookcases containing antique books belonging to Bunny's husband, a collector and book dealer. The top has a pair of wired candlesticks and Staffordshire porcelain.

ABOVE: A black lacquer Regency table.

ABOVE: A French cast figure.

LEFT: The breakfast room is decorated with a Meissen chandelier, French console table, painted French chairs, and a hand-painted sisal carpet that, together with the painted wallpaper, create a cheerful atmosphere.

BEBE WINKLER

Fashionable tailoring

If attention to details is next to godliness, then Bebe Winkler is a decorator of "heavenly" stature. Bebe's attention to quality is uncompromising. The fine lacquer cabinetry she has built for her clients is not just for show. Drawers glide effortlessly; cabinet doors close perfectly. She builds a total environment that is not only concerned with appearances, but with seamless living. Bebe's rooms have a peaceful quality. Everything is in its place, colors are comfortable on the eyes, textures are sleek and yet warm.

Born in Brooklyn, on March 6, 1934, Bebe is the daughter of a traveling salesman for the fashion industry. Her mother, whom she greatly admires, was very organized and had great taste. Bebe's family has its roots in the fashion business. In addition to her father's position on the sales side of the dress business, her grandmother designed dresses during the 1930s. Her aunt was a hat designer, who was well known during the thirties and forties.

Bebe grew up in the Long Island suburb of Hewlett. She started working at eighteen, never attending college. She had a variety of jobs, ranging from working at a travel agency to typing. She finally landed a position at a Seventh Avenue fashion house, eventually becoming the firm's showroom model. That started a new career for her. In the 1960s she worked steadily as a model.

LEFT: Bebe Winkler and Bam Bam in her "yet to be decorated" living room. RIGHT: Bebe designed this living room and recently performed a "touch up" Rich contrasts are created with a French needlepoint rug placed over the wall-to-wall carpeting, an assortment of sofa cushions, floral patterned drapes, and trimmed lampshades. The handpainted screen and side table and the English and French chairs, together with the contemporary glass tables and magazine stands, Czechoslovakian amber glass covered dishes, and a Russian bronze dancer mounted on marble provide a wealth of detail, enhancing the overall quality of this sunny, inviting room.

By accident, she met a woman in the decorating business. They became fast friends. The woman asked Bebe to help her with her design work. Bebe finally left modeling in 1969 to join her friend's business full-time. It was a learning experience. When she finally went solo, Bebe was a full-fledged decorator.

Bebe learned a valuable lesson the time she designed a beautiful glass table top. Her drawing specified an eight-foot length. The client's apartment was on the twenty-fifth floor of a high-rise building. Of course, when the time came to deliver the table, it didn't fit in the elevator. Since that day, Bebe always measures every door and every elevator.

Bebe is thoroughly devoted to her clients. This attention to her projects has made it impossible for her to design her own apartment in Manhattan. "I'm like a shoemaker without any shoes," she quips, adding that her own home will eventually get done. In the meantime she has been busy designing a line of linens, decorative accessories, cushions, and shawls to be marketed as her signature line. And her decorating installations continue, giving clients—who usually end up becoming good friends—modern and comfortable houses and apartments.

DIRECTORY

KALEF ALATON
New York Representative
Marjorie Shushan
30 East 65th Street
New York, NY 10021
(212)570-0338

Los Angeles
(Furniture line only)
Ralph Webb
KA Custom Design
882 North Doheny Drive
Los Angeles, CA 90069

RONALD BRICKE
333 East 69th Street
New York, NY 10021
(212)472-9006

MARIO BUATTA
120 East 80th Street
New York, NY 10021
(212)988-6811

PETER CARLSON
196 Grand Street
New York, NY 10013
(212)925-2173

MADELEINE CASTAING
21 rue Bonaparte
75006 Paris
43 54 91 71

FRANÇOIS CATROUX
20 Faubourg Saint-Honoré
75008 Paris
42 66 69 25

DAVID ANTHONY EASTON
323 East 58th Street
New York, NY 10022
(212)486-6704

ELIZABETH GAROUSTE MATTIA BONETTI
1 rue Oberkampf
75011 Paris
48 05 86 51
37 48 47 18

CHRISTOPHE GOLLUT
116 Fulham Road
London, SW3
(01)370-4101

JACQUES GRANGE
18 rue Servandoni
75006 Paris
47 42 47 34

FRANK GRILL
179 Albion Street
Surrey Hills, NSW 2010
Australia
(02)331-5183

ALBERT HADLEY
Parish-Hadley Associates, Inc.
305 East 63rd Street
New York, NY 10021
(212) 888-7979

GARY HAGER
Parish-Hadley Associates, Inc.
305 East 63rd Street
New York, NY 10021
(212)888-7979

ANTHONY HAIL
1055 Green Street
San Francisco, CA 94133
(415)928-3500

MARK HAMPTON
654 Madison Avenue
New York, NY 10021
(212)753-4110

NICHOLAS HASLAM
105 Kensington Church
Street
London, W87 LN
(01)229-1145

DAVID HICKS
4A Barley Mow Passage
Chiswick
London W4 4PH
(01)994-9222

WILLIAM HODGINS
232 Clarendon Street
Boston, MA 02116
(617)262-9538

NANCY HUANG
211 West 61st Street
New York, NY 10023
(212)489-7848

JED JOHNSON
Jed Johnson,
Alan Wanzenberg
& Associates, Inc.
211 West 61st Street
New York, NY 10023
(212)489-7840

TESSA KENNEDY
Tessa Kennedy Design
Studio 5
9197 Freson Road
London, W11 4BD
(01)221-4546

DAVID KLEINBERG
Parish-Hadley Associates, Inc.
305 East 63rd Street
New York, NY 10021
(212)888-7979

MICHAEL KRIEGER
A. Michael Krieger Interior
Design
45-17 21st Street
Long Island City, NY 11101
(718)706-0077

MICHAEL LA ROCCA
Michael La Rocca, Inc.
150 East 58th Street,
Suite 351
New York, NY 10055
(212)755-5558

ANN LECONEY
755 Park Avenue
New York, NY 10021
(212)472-1265

DANIELA LEUSCH
Via Bigli 15
20121 Milan
(02)784-483

BRIAN McCARTHY
Parish-Hadley Associates, Inc.
305 East 63rd Street
New York, NY 10021
(212)888-7979

ROBERT METZGER
Robert Metzger Interiors
215 East 58th Street
New York, NY 10022
(212)371-9800

JUAN PABLO MOLYNEUX
29 East 69th Street
New York, NY 10021
(212)628-0097

RENZO MONGIARDINO
Viale Bianca Maria 45
20121 Milan
(02)790-131

JUAN MONTOYA
Juan Montoya Design
Corporation
80 8th Avenue, 16th Floor
New York, NY 10011
(212)242-3622

SANDRA NUNNERLEY
Sandra Nunnerley, Inc.
400 East 55th Street
New York, NY 10022
(212)593-1497

SISTER PARISH
Parish-Hadley Associates, Inc.
305 East 63rd Street
New York, NY 10021
(212)888-7979

DANIEL PASSEGRIMAUD
11 rue Princesse
75006 Paris
46 33 40 27
46 33 53 95

NICHOLAS MILES PENTECOST
Nicholas Miles Pentecost
Incorporated
200 East 61st Street
New York, NY 10021
(212)750-1915

JOSEF PRICCI
Josef Pricci, Ltd.
970 Park Avenue
New York, NY 10028
(212)744-4962

JOHN SALADINO
John F. Saladino, Inc.
305 East 63rd Street
New York, NY 10021
(212)752-2440

DAVID SALOMON
508 West End Avenue
New York, NY 10024
(212)874-2695

HENRI SAMUEL
118 Faubourg Saint-Honoré
75008 Paris
42 66 67 92
45 62 38 18

BETTY SHERRILL
McMillen & Co.
155 East 56th Street
New York, NY 10022
(212)753-6377

STEPHEN SILLS
Stephen Sills, Incorporated
204 East 90th Street
New York, NY 10128
(212)289-8180

PAUL SISKIN PERUCHO VALLS
Siskin-Valls, Inc.
21 West 58th Street, 2A
New York, NY 10019
(212)752-3790

ETHEL SMITH
McMillen & Co.
155 East 56th Street
New York, NY 10022
(212)753-6377

JEROME SUTTER
Jerome Sutter Consultants,
Incorporated
1167 Second Avenue
New York, NY 10021
(212)688-7838

DADDO TORRIGIANI
Via Tiziano, 9
20145 Milan
(02)498-5967

HERBERT WELLS
23 West Oak Drive
Houston, Texas 77056
(713)626-1500

BUNNY WILLIAMS
Bunny Williams, Incorporated
4 East 77th Street
New York, NY 10021-1769
(212)772-8585

BEBE WINKLER
Bebe Winkler Interior Design
135 East 55th Street
New York, NY 10022
(212)838-3356